The Gift of
Black Folk

The Gift of
Black Folk

W.E.B. Du Bois

MINT EDITIONS

The Gift of Black Folk was first published in 1924.

This edition published by Mint Editions 2021.

ISBN 9781513282640 | E-ISBN 9781513287669

Published by Mint Editions®

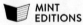 MINT
EDITIONS

minteditionbooks.com

Publishing Director: Jennifer Newens
Design & Production: Rachel Lopez Metzger
Project Manager: Micaela Clark
Typesetting: Westchester Publishing Services

Contents

Foreword

It is not uncommon for casual thinkers to assume that the United States of America is practically a continuation of English nationality. Our speech is English and the English played so large a part in our beginnings that it is easy to fall more or less consciously into the thought that the history of this nation has been but a continuation and development of these beginnings. A little reflection, however, quickly convinces us that at least there was present French influence in the Mississippi Valley and Spanish influence in the southeast and southwest. Everything else however that has been added to the American nationality is often looked upon as a sort of dilution of more or less doubtful value: peoples that had to be assimilated as far as possible and made over to the original and basic type. Thus we continually speak of Germans and Scandinavians, of Irish and Jews, Poles, Austrians and Hungarians; and, with few exceptions, we regard the coming of the Negroes as an unmitigated error and a national liability.

It is high time that this course of our thinking should be changed. America is conglomerate. This is at once her problem and her glory—perhaps indeed her sole and greatest reason for being. Her physical foundation is not English and while it is primarily it is not entirely European. It represents peculiarly a coming together of the peoples of the world. American institutions have been borrowed from England and France in the main, but with contributions from many and widely scattered groups. American history has no prototype and has been developed from the various racial elements. Despite the fact that our mother tongue is called English we have developed an American speech with its idiosyncrasies and idioms, a speech whose purity is not to be measured by its conformity to the speech of the British Isles. And finally the American spirit is a new and interesting result of divers threads of thought and feeling coming not only from America but from Europe and Asia and indeed from Africa.

This essay is an attempt to set forth more clearly than has hitherto been done the effect which the Negro has had upon American life. Its thesis is that despite slavery, war and caste, and despite our present Negro problem, the American Negro is and has been a distinct asset to this country and has brought a contribution without which America could not have been; and that perhaps the essence of our so-called

Negro problem is the failure to recognize this fact and to continue to act as though the Negro was what we once imagined and wanted to imagine him—a representative of a subhuman species fitted only for subordination.

A moment's thought will easily convince open minded persons that the contribution of the Negro to American nationality as slave, freedman and citizen was far from negligible. No element in American life has so subtly and yet clearly woven itself into the warp and woof of our thinking and acting as the American Negro. He came with the first explorers and helped in exploration. His labor was from the first the foundation of the American prosperity and the cause of the rapid growth of the new world in economic and social importance. Modern democracy rests not simply on the striving white men in Europe and America but also on the persistent struggle of the black men in America for two centuries. The military defense of this land has depended upon Negro soldiers from the time of the Colonial wars down to the struggle of the World War. Not only does the Negro appear, reappear and persist in American literature but a Negro American literature has arisen of deep significance, and Negro folk lore and music are among the choicest heritages of this land.

Finally the Negro had played a peculiar spiritual rôle in America as a sort of living, breathing test of our ideals and an example of the faith, hope and tolerance of our religion.

Prescript

Who made America? Who made this land that swings its empire from the Atlantic to the Sea of Peace and from Snow to Fire—this realm of New Freedom, with Opportunity and Ideal unlimited?

Now that its foundations are laid, deep but bare, there are those as always who would forget the humble builders, toiling wan mornings and blazing noons, and picture America as the last reasoned blossom of mighty ancestors; of those great and glorious world builders and rulers who know and see and do all things forever and ever, amen! How singular and blind! For the glory of the world is the possibilities of the commonplace and America is America even because it shows, as never before, the power of the common, ordinary, unlovely man. This is real democracy and not that vain and eternal striving to regard the world as the abiding place of exceptional genius with great black wastes of hereditary idiots.

We who know may not forget but must forever spread the splendid sordid truth that out of the most lowly and persecuted of men, Man made America. And that what Man has here begun with all its want and imperfection, with all its magnificent promise and grotesque failure will some day blossom in the souls of the Lowly.

I

The Black Explorers

How the Negro helped in the discovery of America and gave his ancient customs to the land.

Garcia de Montalvo published in 1510 a Spanish romance which said: "Know ye that on the right hand of the Indies there is an island called California very near the Terrestrial Paradise which is peopled with black women without any men among them, because they were accustomed to live after the fashion of the Amazons. They were of strong and hardy bodies, of ardent courage and of great force."[1]

The legend that the Negro race had touched America even before the day of Columbus rests upon a certain basis of fact: First, the Negro countenance, clear and unmistakable, occurs repeatedly in Indian carvings, among the relics of the Mound Builders and in Mexican temples.[2] Secondly, there are evidences of Negro customs among the Indians in their religious worship; in their methods of building defenses such as the mounds probably were; and particularly in customs of trade. Columbus said that he had been told of a land southwest of the Cape Verde Islands where the black folk had been trading and had used in their trade the well known African alloy of gold called guanin.[3]

"There can be no question whatever as to the reality of the statement in regard to the presence in America of the African pombeiros[4] previous to Columbus because the guani is a Mandingo word and the very alloy

---

1. From a Spanish Romance called *La Sergas de Espladian*, by Garcia de Montalvo, published in 1510; translated in Beasley's *The Negro Trail Blazers of California*, p. 18.
2. Cf. Wiener, *Africa and the Discovery of America*, Vol. 1, pp. 169–70, 172, 174–5; Vol. 3, p. 322; Thurston, *Antiquities of Tennessee*, etc., 1890, p. 105; De Charnay, *Ancient Cities of the New World* (trans. by Gonino and Conant, 1887), pp. 132ff.; Kabell, *America för Columbus*, 1892, p. 235.
3. J. B. Thacher, *Christopher Columbus*, 1903, Vol. 2, pp. 379–80; *Raccolta di documenti e studi publicati dalla R. Commissione Colombiana pel quorto centenario dalla scoperta dell' America*, parte I, Rome, 1892, Vol. 1, p. 96.
4. i. e., Negro Traders.

is of African origin. In 1501 a law was passed forbidding persons to sell guanin to the Indians of Hispaniola."[5]

Wiener thinks "The presence of Negroes with their trading masters in America before Columbus is proved by the representation of Negroes in American sculpture and design, by the occurrence of a black nation at Darien early in the 16th century, but more specifically by Columbus' emphatic reference to Negro traders from Guinea, who trafficked in a gold alloy, guanin, of precisely the same composition and bearing the same name, as frequently referred to by early writers in Africa."[6]

And thirdly, many of the productions of America which have hitherto been considered as indigenous and brought into use especially by the Indians, may easily have been African in origin, as for instance, tobacco, cotton, sweet potatoes and peanuts. It is quite possible that many if not all of these came through the African Negro, being in some cases indigenous to Negro Africa and in other cases transmitted from the Arabs by the Negroes. Tobacco particularly was known in Africa and is mentioned in early America continually in connection with the Negroes. All of these things were spread in America along the same routes starting with the mingling of Negroes and Indians in the West Indies and coming up through Florida and on to Canada. The Arawak Indians, who especially show the effects of contact with Negroes, and fugitive Negroes, together with Negroid Caribs, migrated northward and it was they who led Ponce de Leon to search for the Fountain Bimini where old men became young.[7]

Oviedo says that the sweet potato "came with that evil lot of Negroes and it has taken very well and it is profitable and good sustenance for the Negroes of whom there is a greater number than is necessary on account of their rebellions."[8] In the same way maize and sugar cane may have been imported from Africa.

Further than this the raising of bread roots, manioc, yam and sweet potatoes may have come to America from Guinea by way of Brazil. From Brazil the culture of these crops spread and many of the words referring to them are of undoubted African origin.

---

5. Thacher, Vol. 2, pp. 379, 380; Wiener, Vol. 2, pp. 116–17.

6. Wiener, Vol. 3, p. 365.

7. *Memoir of Hernando de Essalante Fontanedo, respecting Florida,* translated from the Spanish by Buckingham Smith, Washington, 1854.

8. Oviedo y Valdes, *Historia general,* etc., Vol. 1, p. 286.

Negroes probably reached the eastern part of South America from the West Indies while others from the same source went north along the roads marked by the Mound Builders as far as Canada.

"The chief cultural influence of the Negro in America was exerted by a Negro colony in Mexico, most likely from Teotihuacan and Tuxtla, who may have been instrumental in establishing the city of Mexico. From here their influence pervaded the neighboring tribes and ultimately, directly or indirectly, reached Peru."[9]

The mounds of the "Mound Builders" were probably replicas of Negro forts in Africa. "That this tendency to build forts and stockades proceeded from the Antilles, whence the Arawaks had come in the beginning of the sixteenth century, is proved by the presence of similar works in Cuba. These are found in the most abandoned and least-explored part of the island and there can be little doubt that they were locations of fugitive Negro and Indian stockades, precisely such as were in use in Africa. It is not possible to prove the direct participation of the Negroes in the fortifications of the North American Indians, but as the civilizing influence on the Indians to a great extent proceeded from Cuba over Florida towards the Huron Country in the north, the solution of the question of the Mound Builders is to be looked for in the perpetuation of Arawak or Carib methods, acquired from the Negroes, as well attested by Ovando's complaint in 1503 that the Negroes spoiled the manners of the Indians; and transferred to the white traders, who not only adopted the methods of the Indians, but frequently lived among the Indians as part of them, especially in Brazil where we have ample documentary evidence of the fact."[10]

All this is prehistoric and in part conjectural and yet it seems reasonable to suppose that much in custom, trade and religion which has been regarded as characteristic of the American Indian arose from strong Negro influences of the pre-Columbian period.

After the discovery of America by Columbus many Negroes came with the early explorers. Many of these early black men were civilized Christians and sprung from the large numbers of Negroes imported into Spain and Portugal during the fifteenth century, where they replaced as laborers the expelled Moors. Afterward came the mass of slaves brought by the direct African slave trade.

---

9. Wiener, Vol. 3, p. 365.
10. Wiener, Vol. 1, p. 190.

From the beginning of the fifteenth century mention of the Negro in America becomes frequent. In 1501 they were permitted to enter the colonies; in 1503 the Governor of Hispaniola sought to prohibit their transportation to America because they fled to the Indians and taught them bad manners. By 1506 they were coming again because the work of one Negro was worth more than that of four Indians. In 1518 the new sugar culture in Spain and the Canary Islands began to be transferred to the West Indies and Negroes were required as laborers. In 1521 Negroes were not to be used on errands because they incited Indians to rebellion and the following year they rose in rebellion on Diego Columbus' mill. In 1540, in Quivera, Mexico, there was a Negro priest and in 1542 there were at Guamango, Mexico, three Brotherhoods of the True Cross of Spaniards, one of which was of Negroes and one of Indians.

Thus the Negro is seen not only entering as a laborer but becoming a part of the civilization of the New World. Helps says: "Very early in the history of the American Continent there are circumstances to show that Negroes were gradually entering into that part of the New World. They constantly appear at remarkable points in the narrative. When the Marquis Pizarro had been slain by the conspirators, his body was dragged to the Cathedral by two Negroes. The murdered Factor, Illan Suarez, was buried by Negroes and Indians. After the battle of Anaquito, the head of the unfortunate Viceroy, Blasco Nunez Vela, was cut off by a Negro. On the outbreak of the great earthquake at Guatemala, the most remarkable figure in that night's terrors was a gigantic Negro, who was seen in many parts of the city, and who assisted no one, however much he was implored. In the narrative of the return of Las Casas to his diocese, it has been seen that he was attended by a Negro. And many other instances might be adduced, showing that, in the decade from 1535 to 1545, Negroes had come to form part of the household of the wealthier colonists. At the same time, in the West Indian Islands which had borne the first shock of the conquest, and where the Indians had been more swiftly destroyed, the Negroes were beginning to form the bulk of the population; and the licenses for importation were steadily increasing in number."[11]

Continually they appear with the explorers. Nuflo de Olana, a Negro, was with Balboa when he discovered the Pacific Ocean,[12] and

---

11. Helps, *Spanish Conquest in America*, Vol. 4, p. 401.
12. J. F. Rippy in *Journal of Negro History*, Vol. 6, p. 183.

afterward thirty Negroes helped Balboa direct the work of over 500 Indians in transporting the material for his ships across the mountains to the South Sea.[13]

Cortes carried Negroes and Indians with him from Cuba to Mexico and one of these Negroes was the first to sow and reap grain in Mexico. There were two Negroes with Velas in 1520 and 200 black slaves with Alvarado on his desperate expedition to Quito. Almagro and Valdivia in 1525 were saved from death by Negroes.[14]

As early as 1528 there were about 10,000 Negroes in the New World. We hear of one sent as an agent of the Spanish to burn a native village in Honduras. In 1539 they accompanied De Soto and one of them stayed among the Indians in Alabama and became the first settler from the old world. In 1555 in Santiago de Chile a free Negro owns land in the town. Menendez had a company of trained Negro artisans and agriculturalists when he founded St. Augustine in 1565 and in 1570 Negroes founded the town of Santiago del Principe.

In most of these cases probably leadership and initiative on the part of the early Negro pioneers in America was only spasmodic or a matter of accident. But this was not always true and there is one well-known case which, despite the propaganda of 400 years, survives as a clear and important instance of Negro leadership in exploration. This is the romantic story of Stephen Dorantes or as he is usually called, Estevanico, who sailed from Spain in 1527 with the expedition of Panfilo de Narvaez.[15] This fleet of five vessels and 600 colonists and soldiers started from Cuba and landed in Tampa Bay in 1582. But disaster followed disaster until at last there were but four survivors of whom one was Estevanico "an Arab Negro from Azamor on the Atlantic coast of Morocco"; he is elsewhere described as "black" and a "person of intelligence." Besides him there was his master Dorantes and two other Spaniards, de Vaca and Maldonado.[16] For six years these men

---

13. Helps, Vol. 1, p. 421.

14. Rippy, *loc. cit.*

15. The following narrative is based on: H. O. Flipper, *Did a Negro discover Arizona and New Mexico* (contains a translation of parts of the narrative of Pedro de Castaneda de Majera); Pedro de Castaneda, "Account of the Expedition to Cibola which took place in the year 1540. . ." translated in *Spanish Explorers in the Southern United States* (J. F. Jameson Ed.); Beasley, *Trail Blazers of California,* Chapter 2; Rippy, in *Journal of Negro History,* Vol. 6, pp. 183ff.; *American Anthropologist,* Vol. 4.

16. A fifth survivor, a Spaniard, stayed with the Indiana and was afterward found by DeSoto.

maintained themselves by practicing medicine among the Indians, and were the first to reach Mexico from Florida by the overland route.

Estevanico and de Vaca went forward to meet the outposts of the Spaniards established in Mexico. Estevanico returned with an escort and brought on the other two men. The four then went west to the present Mexican cities, Chihuahua and Sonora and reached Culiacan, the capital of the state of Sinaloa, in April, 1536.

Coronado was governor of Sinaloa and on hearing the story of the wanderers, he immediately hastened with them to the viceroy, Mendoza, in the city of Mexico. They told the viceroy not only of their own adventures but what they had heard of the rich lands toward the North and of the cities with houses four and five stories high which were really the Pueblos of New Mexican Indians. Mendoza was eager to explore these lands. He had already heard something about them and he and Cortes had planned to make the exploration together but could not agree upon terms. Cortes therefore hurried to fit out a small fleet in 1537. He took 400 Spaniards and 300 Negroes, sailed up the Gulf of California and called the country "California". He then returned to Spain for the last time.

Meantime, de Vaca and Maldonado after several unsuccessful attempts also went to Spain leaving Dorantes and Estevanico. Dorantes refused to take part in the proposed expedition to the North but sold his slave Estevanico to Mendoza. Certain Franciscan Monks joined the expedition and Fray Marcos de Niza became the leader, having already had some experience in exploration in Peru. Estevanico, because of his knowledge of the Indian language and especially of the sign language, was the guide, and the party started North for what the viceroy dreamed were the Seven Cities of Cibola. They left March 7th, 1539, and arrived at Vacapa in central Sinaloa on the 21st. Fray Marcos, probably from timidity, sent Estevanico on ahead with an escort of Indians whom he could send back as messengers.[17] The Negro marked his journey by large wooden crosses and in this way with Estevanico far ahead they traveled for two weeks until suddenly Fray Marcos was met by a fleeing band of badly frightened Indians who told him that Estevanico had reached Cibola and had been killed. Fray Marcos named the country "El Nueva Reyno de San Francisco" but being himself scared, distributed among the Indians everything which his party had in their packs, except the

---

17. Another story is that Estevanico and the Monks did not get on well together.

vestments for saying Mass, and traveling by double marches, returned to Mexico.

Meantime let us follow the adventure of Estevanico: Knowing how much depended upon appearance in that unknown and savage land, Estevanico traveled in magnificence, decorated with bells and feathers and carrying a symbolic gourd which was recognized among the Indian tribes thereabouts as a symbol of authority. When he reached the Pueblos, the Indian chiefs were in a quandary. First of all they recognized in Estevanico's retinue, numbers of their ancient Indian enemies. Secondly, they were frightened because Estevanico informed them "that two white men were coming behind him who had been sent by a great Lord and knew about the things in the sky and that they were coming to instruct them in divine matters." They had good reason to fear that this meant the onslaught of some powerful enemy. And, moreover, they were puzzled because this black man came as a representative of white men: "The Lord of Cibola, inquiring of him whether he had other brethren, he answered that he had an infinite number and that they had a great store of weapons with them and that they were not very far thence. When they heard this, many of the chief men consulted together and resolved to kill him that he might not give news unto these brethren where they dwelt[18] and that for this cause they slew him and cut him into many pieces, which were divided among all the chief Lords that they might know assuredly that he was dead. . ."

This climax is still told in a legend current among the Zuni Indians today: "It is to be believed that a long time ago, when roofs lay over the walls of Kya-ki-me, when smoke hung over the housetops, and the ladder rounds were still unbroken in Kya-ki-me, then the black Mexicans came from their abodes in Everlasting Summerland. One day, unexpectedly, out of Hemlock Canon they came, and descended to Kya-ki-me. But when they said they would enter the covered way, it seems that our ancients looked not gently at them; for with these black Mexicans came many Indians of So-no-li, as they call it now, . . . who were enemies of our ancients. Therefore, these our ancients, being always bad-tempered, and quick to anger, made fools of themselves after their fashion, rushing into their town and out of their town, shouting, skipping and shooting with their sling-stones and arrows and tossing their war-clubs. Then the Indians of So-no-li set up a great howl, and thus they and our ancients

---

18. The story that Estevanico was killed because of his greed is evidently apocryphal.

W.E.B. DU BOIS

did much ill to one another. Then and thus was killed by our ancients, right where the stone stands down by the arroyo of Kya-ki-me, one of the black Mexicans, a large man with chilli lips (i. e., lips swollen from eating chilli peppers) and some of the Indians they killed, catching others. Then the rest ran away, chased by our grandfathers, and went back toward their country in the Land of Everlasting Summer. . ."[19]

The village reached by Estevanico was Hawikih as it was called by the Indians and Grenada as the Spaniards named it. It is fifteen miles southwest of the present village of Zuni and is thus within New Mexico and east of the boundary between New Mexico and Arizona. Thus Estevanico was the first European to discover Arizona and New Mexico. Fray Marcos returned with Coronado and came as far as the village in 1540 while Mendoza sent others to pursue explorations that same year within the present confines of Arizona and they brought back various stories of the death of Estevanico.

After that for 40 years explorations rested until 1582 when again the Spaniards entered the territory. With all the Spanish explorers in Florida, Texas, Arizona, New Mexico and Kansas, there were Negro slaves and helpers but none with the initiative, perseverance and success of Estevanico.

In the after pioneering that took place in later days in the great western wilderness, the Negro was often present. There was a black man with Lewis and Clark in 1804; Jacob Dodson, a free Negro of Washington, volunteered to accompany Fremont in his California expedition of 1843. He was among the 25 persons selected by Fremont to accompany him in the discovery of Clamath Lake and also in his ride from Los Angeles to Monterey. Among the early settlers of California coming up from Mexico were many Negroes and mulattoes.[20]

William Alexander Leidsdroff was the most distinguished Negro pioneer of California and at one time lived in the largest house in San Francisco. He owned the first steamship sailing in San Francisco Bay, and was a prominent business man, a member of the City Council and treasurer and member of the school committee. H. H. Bancroft says: "William Alexander Leidsdroff, a native of Danish West Indies, son of a Dane by a mulattress, who came to the United States as a boy

---

19. Legends of the Zuni Pueblos of New Mexico quoted in Lowery *Spanish Settlements in the United States,* 1513–1561, pp. 281–82.
20. Cf. Beasley, Chapter 10.

and became a master of vessels sailing between New York and New Orleans, came to California as manager of the 'Julia Ann,' on which he made later trips to the Islands, down to 1845." His correspondence from 1845, when he became United States Vice-Consul is a valuable source of historical information. Many Negroes came in the rush of the "forty-niners" as pioneers and miners as well as slaves.

The Negro's work as a pioneer extends down until our day. The late Commodore Peary who discovered the North Pole said: "Matthew A. Henson, my Negro assistant, has been with me in one capacity or another since my second trip to Nicaragua in 1887. I have taken him on each and all of my expeditions, except the first, and also without exception on each of my farthest sledge trips. This position I have given him primarily because of his adaptability and fitness for the work, and secondly on account of his loyalty. He is a better dog driver and can handle a sledge better than any man living, except some of the best Esquimo hunters themselves." This leaves Henson today as the only living human being who has stood at the North Pole.

II

BLACK LABOR

How the Negro gave his brawn and brain to fell the forests, till the soil and make America a rich and prosperous land.

The primary reason for the presence of the black man in America was, of course, his labor and much has been written of the influence of slavery as established by the Portuguese, Spanish, Dutch and English. Most writers have written of slavery as a moral and economic evil or of the worker, white and black, as a victim of this system. In this chapter, however, let us think of the slave as a laborer, as one who furnished the original great labor force of the new world and differed from modern labor only in the wages received, the political and civil rights enjoyed, and the cultural surroundings from which he was taken.

Negro labor has played a peculiar and important part in the history of the modern world. The black man was the pioneer in the hard physical work which began the reduction of the American wilderness and which not only hastened the economic development of America directly but indirectly released for other employment, thousands of white men and thus enabled America to grow economically and spiritually at a rate previously unparalleled anywhere in history. It was black labor that established the modern world commerce which began first as a commerce in the bodies of the slaves themselves and was the primary cause of the prosperity of the first great commercial cities of our day. Then black labor was thrown into the production of four great crops—tobacco, sugar, rice and cotton. These crops were not new but their production on a large cheap scale was new and had a special significance because they catered to the demands of the masses of men and thus made possible an interchange of goods such as the luxury trade of the Middle Ages catering to the rich could not build. Black labor, therefore, beneath these crops became an important part of the Industrial Revolution of the eighteenth and nineteenth centuries.

Moreover the black slave brought into common labor certain new spiritual values not yet fully realized. As a tropical product with a sensuous receptivity to the beauty of the world he was not as easily reduced to be the mechanical draft-horse which the northern European laborer became. He was not easily brought to recognize any ethical sanctions in work as such but tended to work as the results pleased him and refused to work or sought to refuse when he did not find the spiritual returns adequate; thus he was easily accused of laziness and driven as a slave when in truth he brought to modern manual labor a renewed valuation of life.

The Negro worked as farm hand and peasant proprietor, as laborer, artisan and inventor and as servant in the house, and without him, America as we know it, would have been impossible.

The numerical growth of the Negro population in America indicates his economic importance. The exact number of slaves exported to America will never be known. Probably 25,000 Negroes a year arrived in America between 1698 and 1707. After 1713 this rose to 30,000 and by 1775 to over 40,000 a year. The American Revolution stopped the trade, but it was revived afterward and reached enormous proportions. One estimate is that a million Negroes came in the sixteenth century, three million in the seventeenth, seven million in the eighteenth and four million in the nineteenth or fifteen million in all. Certainly at least ten million came and this meant sixty million killed and stolen in Africa because of the methods of capture and the horror of the middle passage. This, with the Asiatic trade, cost black Africa a hundred million souls.[1] Bancroft places the total slave population of the continental colonies at 59,000 in 1714, 78,000 in 1727, and 293,000 in 1754.

In the West Indies the whole laboring population early became Negro or Negro with an infiltration of Indian and white blood. In the United States at the beginning of our independent national existence, Negroes formed a fifth of the population of the whole nation. The exact figures are:[2]

Percentage Negro in the Population

	United States	South
1920	9.9	26.1
1910	10.7	29.8
1900	11.6	32.3
1890	11.9	33.8

1. Cf. Du Bois, *Suppression of the Slave Trade;* Du Bois, *The Negro* (Home University Library).

2. United States Census, *Negro Population 1790–1915;* Fourteenth Census, Vol. 3.

1880	13.1	36.0
1870	12.7	36.0
1860	14.1	36.8
1850	15.7	37.3
1840	16.8	38.0
1830	18.1	37.9
1820	18.4	37.2
1810	19.0	36.7
1800	18.9	35.0
1790	19.3	35.2

If we consider the number of Negroes for each 1,000 whites, we have:

1920	110	369
1910	120	426
1900	132	480
1890	136	512
1880	152	564
1870	145	562
1860	165	582
1850	186	595
1840	203	613
1830	221	610
1820	225	592
1810	235	579
1800	233	539
1790	239	543

The proportion of Negroes in the North was small, falling from 3.4% in 1790 to 1.8% in 1910. Nevertheless even here the indirect influence of the Negro worker was large. The trading colonies, New England and New York, built up a lucrative commerce based largely on the results of his toil in the South and in the West Indies, and this commerce supported local agriculture and manufacture. I have said in my *Suppression of the Slave Trade:* "Vessels from Massachusetts, Rhode Island, Connecticut, and, to a less extent from New Hampshire, were early and largely engaged in the carrying slave-trade. 'We know,' said Thomas Pemberton in 1795, 'that a large trade to Guinea was carried on for many years by the citizens of Massachusetts Colony, who were the proprietors of the vessels and their cargoes, out and home. Some of the slaves purchased in Guinea, and I suppose the greatest part of them, were sold in the West Indies.' Dr. John Eliot asserted that 'it made a considerable branch of our commerce. . . It declined very little until the Revolution.' Yet the trade of this colony was said not to equal that of Rhode Island. Newport was the mart for slaves offered for sale in the North, and a point of reshipment for all slaves. It was principally this trade that raised Newport to her commercial importance in the eighteenth century. Connecticut, too, was an important slave-trader, sending large numbers of horses and other commodities to the West Indies in exchange for slaves, and selling the slaves in other colonies."

"This trade formed a perfect circle. Owners of slavers carried slaves to South Carolina, and brought home naval stores for their ship-building; or to the West Indies and brought home molasses; or to other colonies, and brought home hogsheads. The molasses was made into the highly prized New England rum, and shipped in these hogsheads to Africa for more slaves. Thus the rum-distilling industry indicated to some extent the activity of New England in the slave-trade. In May, 1752, one Captain Freeman found so many slavers fitting out that, in spite of the large importations of molasses, he could get no rum for his vessel. In Newport alone twenty-two stills were at one time running continuously; and Massachusetts annually distilled 15,000 hogsheads of molasses into this 'chief manufacture.'"[3]

In New York and New Jersey Negroes formed between 7 and 8% of the total population in 1790, which meant that they were probably 25% of the labor force of those colonies, especially on the farms.

The growth of the great slave crops shows the increasing economic value of Negro labor. In 1619, 20,000 pounds of tobacco went from Virginia to England. Just before the Revolutionary War, 100 million pounds a year were being sent, and at the beginning of the twentieth century, 800 millions were raised in the United States alone. Sugar was a luxury for the rich and physicians until the eighteenth century, when it began to pour out of the West Indies. By the middle of the nineteenth century a million tons of cane sugar were raised each year and this had increased to nearly 3 millions in 1900. The cotton crop rose correspondingly. England, the chief customer at first, consumed 13,000

---

3. Du Bois, *Suppression of the Slave Trade*, Chapter 4.

bales in 1781, 572,000 in 1820, 871,000 in 1830 and 3,366,000 in 1860. The United States raised 6 million bales in 1880, and at the beginning of the twentieth century raised 11 million bales annually.

This tremendous increase in crops which formed a large part of modern commerce was due primarily to black labor. At first most of this labor was brute toil of the lowest sort. Our estimate of the value of this work and what it has done for America depends largely upon our estimate of the value of such toil. It must be confessed that, measured in wages and in public esteem, such work stands low in America and in the civilized world. On the other hand the fact that it does stand so low constitutes one of the greatest problems of social advance. Hard manual labor, and much of it of a disagreeable sort, must for a long time lie at the basis of civilized life. We are continually transmitting some of it to machines, but the residuum remains large. In an ideal society it would be highly-paid work because of its unpleasantness and necessity; and even today, no matter what we may say of the individual worker or of the laboring class, we know that the foundation of America is built on the backs of the manual laborer.

This was particularly true in the earlier centuries. The problem of America in the fifteenth and sixteenth centuries was the problem of manual labor. It was settled by importing white bond servants from Europe, and black servants from Africa, and compelling the American Indians to work. Indian slavery failed to play any great part because the comparatively small number of Indians in the West Indies were rapidly killed off by the unaccustomed toil or mingled their blood and pooled their destinies with the Negroes. On the continent, on the other hand, the Indians were too powerful, both in numbers and organization, to be successfully enslaved. The white bond servants and the Negroes therefore became the main laboring force of the new world and with their toil the economic development of the continent began.

There arose a series of special laws to determine the status of laborers which became the basis of the great slave codes. As the free European white artisans poured in, these labor codes gradually came to distinguish between slavery based on race and free labor. The slave codes greatly weakened the family ties and largely destroyed the family as a center of government or of economic organization. They made the plantation the center of economic life and left more or less religious autonomy. They provided punishment by physical torture, death or sale, but they always left some minimum of incentive by which the slave could have the beginnings of private possession.

In this way the economic organization was provided by which the middle classes of the world were supplied with a cheap sweetening material derived from sugar cane; a cheap luxury, tobacco; larger quantities of rice; and finally, and above all, a cheap and universal material for clothing, cotton. These were things that all men wanted who had anything to offer in labor or materials for the satisfaction of their wants. The cost of raising them was a labor cost almost entirely because land in America was at that time endless in fertility and extent. The old world trade therefore which sought luxuries in clothing, precious metal and stones, spices, etc., for the rich, transformed itself to a world-wide trade in necessities incomparably richer and bigger than its medieval predecessor because of its enormous basis of demand. Its first appearance was in the slave trade where the demand for the new American crops showed itself in a demand for the labor necessary to raise them; thus the slave trade itself was at the bottom of the rise of great commerce, and the beginning of modern international commerce. This trade stimulated invention and was stimulated by it. The wellbeing of European workers increased and their minds were stimulated. Economic and political revolution followed, to which America fell heir. New immigrants poured in. New conceptions of religion, government and work arose and at the bottom of it all and one of its efficient causes was the toil of the increasing millions of black slaves.

As the nation developed this slave labor became confined more and more to the raising of cotton, although sugar continued to be the chief crop in the West Indies and Louisiana, and rice on the southeast coast and tobacco in Virginia. This world importance of cotton brought an economic crisis: Rich land in America, adapted to slave methods of culture, was becoming limited, and must either be increased or slavery would die an economic death. On the other hand, beside the plantation hands, there had grown up a large class of Negro servants and laborers who were distributed both north and south. These laborers in particular came into competition with the white laborer and especially the new immigrants. This and other economic causes led to riots in Philadelphia, New York and Cincinnati and a growing conviction on the part of a newly enfranchised white workingmen that one great obstacle in America was slave labor, together with the necessarily low status of the freedmen. These economic reasons overthrew slavery.[4]

---

4. Cf. Du Bois, *The Philadelphia Negro,* Chapter 4.

W.E.B. DU BOIS

After the legal disappearance of slavery its natural results remained in the mass of freedmen who had been trained in the necessary ignorance and inefficiency of slave labor. On such a foundation it was easy to build and emphasize race prejudice. On the other hand, however, there was still plenty of work for even the ignorant and careless working man, so that the Negro continued to raise cotton and the other great crops and to do throughout the country the work of the unskilled laborer and the servant. He continued to be the main laboring force of the South in industrial lines and began to invade the North.

His full power as a labor reservoir was not seen until the transformation of the World War. In a few short months 500,000 black laborers came North to fill the void made by the stoppage of immigration and the rush of white working men into the munitions industry. This was simply a foretaste of what will continue to happen. The Negro still is the mightiest single group of labor force in the United States. As this labor grows more intelligent, self-conscious and efficient, it will turn to higher and higher grades of work and it will reinforce the workingman's point of view.[5]

It must not be assumed, however, that the labor of the Negro has been simply the muscle-straining unintelligent work of the lowest grade. On the contrary he has appeared both as personal servant, skilled laborer and inventor. That the Negroes of colonial times were not all ignorant savages is shown by the advertisements concerning them. Continually runaway slaves are described as speaking very good English; sometimes as speaking not only English but Dutch and French. Some could read and write and play musical instruments. Others were blacksmiths, limeburners, bricklayers and cobblers. Others were noted as having considerable sums of money.[6] In the early days in the South the whole conduct of the house was in the hands of the Negro house servant; as butler, cook, nurse, valet and maid, the Negro conducted family life.

Thus by social contact and mingling of blood the Negro house servant became closely identified with the civilization of the South and contributed to it in many ways. For a long time before emancipation the house servant had been pushing steadily upward; in many cases he had learned to read and write despite the law. Sometimes he had entered the

---

5. Cf. Woodson, *A Century of Negro Migration;* E. J. Scott: *Negro Migration During the War.*
6. *Journal of Negro History,* Vol. 1, p. 163.

skilled trades and was enabled by hiring his time to earn money of his own and in rare cases to buy his own freedom. Sometimes he was freed and sent North and given money and land; but even when he was in the South and in the family and an ambitious menial, he influenced the language and the imagination of his masters; the children were nursed at the breast of black women, and in daily intercourse the master was thrown in the company of Negroes more often than in the company of white people.

From this servile work there went a natural development. The private cook became the public cook in boarding houses, and restaurant keeper. The butler became the caterer; the "Black Mammy" became the nurse, and the work of all these in their various lines was of great influence. The cooks and caterers led and developed the art of good-eating throughout the South and particularly in cities like New Orleans and Charleston; and in northern cities like Philadelphia and New York their methods of cooking chicken and terrapin, their invention of ice cream and their general good taste set a standard which has seldom been surpassed in the world. Moreover, it gave economic independence to numbers of Negroes. It enabled them to educate their children and it furnished to the abolition movement a class of educated colored people with some money who were able to help. After emancipation these descendants of the house servant became the leading class of American Negroes. Notwithstanding the social stigma connected with menial service and still lingering there, partially because slaves and freedmen were so closely connected with it, it is without doubt one of the most important of the Negro's gifts to America.

During the existence of slavery all credit for inventions was denied the Negro slave as a slave could not take out a patent. Nevertheless Negroes did most of the mechanical work in the South before the Civil War and more than one suggestion came from them for improving machinery. We are told that in Virginia: "The county records of the seventeenth century reveal the presence of many Negro mechanics in the colony during that period, this being especially the case with carpenters and coopers."[7]

As example of slave mechanics it is stated that among the slaves of the first Robert Beverly was a carpenter valued at £30, and that Ralph Wormeley, of Middlesex county, owned a cooper and a carpenter each

---

7. Bruce, *Economic History of Virginia*, Vol. 2, pp. 405–6.

valued at £35. Colonel William Byrd mentions the use of Negroes in iron mining in 1732. In New Jersey slaves were employed as miners, ironworkers, sawmill hands, house and ship carpenters, wheelwrights, coopers, tanners, shoemakers, millers and bakers, among other employments, before the Revolutionary War. As early as 1708 there were enough slave mechanics in Pennsylvania to make the freemen feel their competition severely. In Massachusetts and other states we hear of an occasional artisan.[8]

During the early part of the nineteenth century the Negro artisans increased. The Spanish Governor Salcedo, early in the nineteenth century, in trying to keep the province of Louisiana loyal to Spain, made the militia officers swear allegiance and among them were two companies of colored men from New Orleans "who composed all the mechanics which the city possessed."[9]

Later, black refugees from San Domingo saved Louisiana from economic ruin. Formerly, Louisiana had had prosperous sugar-makers; but these industries had been dead for nearly twenty-five years when the attempt to market sugar was revived. Two Spaniards erected near New Orleans, a distillery and a battery of sugar kettles and began to manufacture rum and syrup. They had little success until Etienne de Boré, a colored San Dominican, appeared. "Face to face with ruin because of the failure of the indigo crop, he staked his all on the granulation of sugar. He enlisted the services of these successful San Dominicans and went to work. In all American history there can be fewer scenes more dramatic than the one described by careful historians of Louisiana, the day when the final test was made and the electrical word was passed around, 'It granulates!'"

De Boré sold $12,000 worth of sugar that year. Agriculture in the Delta began to flourish and seven years later New Orleans was selling 2,000,000 gallons of rum, 250,000 gallons of molasses and 5,000,000 pounds of sugar. It was the beginning of the commercial reign of one of the great commercial cities of America and it started with the black refugees from San Domingo.[10]

In the District of Columbia many "were superior mechanics." Olmsted, in his journeys through the slave states just before the Civil War, found slave artisans in all the states. In Virginia they worked in

8. Atlanta University Publications: Cf. *The Negro Artisan*, 1902–1912, and *Economic Cooperation among Negro Americans*, 1907.
9. Alice Dunbar Nelson in *Journal of Negro History*, Vol. 2, p. 52.
10. Alice Dunbar Nelson, in the *Journal of Negro History*, Vol. 1, p. 375.

tobacco factories, ran steamboats, made barrels, etc. On a South Carolina plantation he was told by the master that the Negro mechanic "exercised as much skill and ingenuity as the ordinary mechanics that he was used to employ in New England." In Charleston and some other places they were employed in cotton factories. In Alabama he saw a black carpenter—careful and accurate calculator and excellent workman; he was bought for $2,000. In Louisiana he was told that master mechanics often bought up slave mechanics and acted as contractors. In Kentucky the slaves worked in factories for hemp-bagging, and in iron work on the Cumberland river, and also in tobacco factories. In the newspapers advertisements for runaway mechanics were often seen, as, for instance a blacksmith in Texas, "very smart"; a mason in Virginia, etc. In Mobile an advertisement read "good blacksmiths and horseshoers for sale on reasonable terms."[11]

Such men naturally showed inventive genius, here and there. There is a strong claim that the real credit for the invention of the cotton gin is due to a Negro on the plantation where Eli Whitney worked. Negroes early invented devices for handling sails, corn harvesters, and an evaporating pan for refining sugar. In the United States patent office there is a record of 1500 inventions made by Negroes and this is only a part of those that should be credited to Negroes as the race of the inventor is not usually recorded.

In 1846 Norbert Rillieux, a colored man of Louisiana, invented and patented a Vacuum pan which revolutionized the method of refining sugar. He was a machinist and engineer of fine reputation, and devised a system of sewerage for New Orleans which the city refused to accept because of his color.

Sydney W. Winslow, president of the United Shoe Machinery Company, laid the foundation of his great organization by the purchase of an invention by a native of Dutch Guiana named Jan E. Matzeliger. Matzeliger was the son of a Negro woman and her husband, a Dutch engineer. He came to America as a young man and worked as a cobbler in Philadelphia and Lynn. He died in 1889 before he had realized the value of his invention.

Matzeliger invented a machine for lasting shoes. It held the shoe on the last, gripped and pulled the leather down around the sole and heel, guided and drove the nails into place and released a completed shoe

---

11. Olmsted, *A Journey in the Seaboard Slave States, Journey through Texas,* and *Journey in the Back Country.*

from the machine. This patent was bought by Mr. Winslow and on it was built the great United Shoe Machinery Company, which now has a capital stock of more than twenty million dollars, and employs over 5,000 operatives in factories covering 20 acres of ground. This business enterprise is one of the largest in our country's industrial development. Since the formation of this company in 1890, the product of American shoe factories has increased from $200,000,000 to $552,631,000, and the exportation of American shoes from $1,000,000 to $11,000,000. This development is due to the superiority of the shoes produced by machines founded on the original Matzeliger type.[12] The cost of shoes has been cut in half, the quality greatly improved, the wages of workers increased, the hours of labor diminished, and all these factors have made "the Americans the best shod people in the world."

After Matzeliger's death his Negro blood was naturally often denied, but in the shoe-making districts the Matzeliger type of machine is still referred to as the "Nigger machine"; or the "Niggerhead" machine; and "A certified copy of the death certificate of Matzeliger, which was furnished the writer by William J. Connery, Mayor of Lynn, on October 23rd, 1912, states that Matzeliger was a mulatto."[13]

Elijah McCoy is the pioneer inventor of automatic lubricators for machinery. He completed and patented his first lubricating cup in 1872 and since then has made some fifty different inventions relating principally to the automatic lubrication of machinery. He is regarded as the pioneer in the art of steadily supplying oil to machinery in intermittent drops from a cup so as to avoid the necessity for stopping the machine to oil it. His lubricating cup was in use for years on stationary and locomotive machinery in the West including the great railway locomotives, the boiler engines of the steamers on the Great Lakes, on transatlantic steamships, and in many of our leading factories. "McCoy's lubricating cups were famous thirty years ago as a necessary equipment in all up-to-date machinery, and it would be rather interesting to know how many of the thousands of machinists who used them daily had any idea then that they were the invention of a colored man."[14]

---

12. Prior to the Matzeliger machine the McKay machine was patented, designed for making the heaviest and cheapest kind of men's shoes. The Matzeliger machine was designed for light work, women's shoes, etc., and was the most important invention necessary to the formation of the United Shoe Machinery Company.

13. H. E. Baker, in *Journal of Negro History*, Vol. 2, pp. 21ff.

14. Baker: *The Colored Inventor*, p. 7.

Another great Negro inventor was Granville T. Woods who patented more than fifty devices relating to electricity. Many of his patents were assigned to the General Electric Company of New York, the Westinghouse Company of Pennsylvania, the American Bell Telephone Company of Boston and the American Engineering Company of New York. His work and that of his brother Liates Wood has been favorably mentioned in technical and scientific journals.

J. H. Dickinson and his son S. L. Dickinson of New Jersey have been granted more than 12 patents for devices connected with player pianos. W. B. Purvis of Philadelphia was an early inventor of machinery for making paper bags. Many of his patents were sold to the Union Paper Bag Company of New York.

Today the Negro is an economic factor in the United States to a degree realized by few. His occupations were thus grouped in 1920:[15]

The men were employed as follows:

in agriculture	1,566,627
in extraction of minerals	72,892
in manufacturing and mechanical industries	781,827
in transportation	308,896
in trade	129,309
in public service	49,586
in professional service	41,056
in domestic and personal service	273,959
in clerical occupations	28,710

The women were employed as follows:

in agriculture	612,261
in manufacturing and mechanical industries	104,983
in trade	11,158
in professional service	39,127
in domestic and personal service	790,631
in clerical occupations	8,301

15. U. S. Census of 1920. Wilcox-Du Bois, *Negroes in the United States* (U. S. Census bulletin No. 8, 1904).

A list of occupations in which at least 10,000 Negroes were engaged in 1920 is impressive:

Males

Farmers	845,299
Farm laborers	664,567
Garden laborers	15,246
Lumber men	25,400
Coal miners	54,432
Masons	10,606
Carpenters	34,217
Firemen (not locomotive)	23,152
Laborers	127,860
Laborers in chemical industries	17,201
Laborers in cigar and tobacco factories	12,951
Laborers in clay, glass and stone industries	18,130
Laborers in food industries	24,638
Laborers in iron and steel industries	104,518
Laborers in lumber and furniture industries	103,154
Laborers in cotton mills	10,182
Laborers in other industries	80,583
Machinists	10,286
Semi-skilled operatives in food industries	11,160
Semi-skilled operatives in iron and steel industries	22,916
Semi-skilled operatives in other industries	14,745
Longshoremen	27,206
Chauffeurs	38,460
Draymen	56,556
Street laborers	35,673
Railway laborers	99,967
Delivery men	24,352
Laborers in coal yards, warehouses, etc.	27,197
Laborers, etc., in stores	39,446
Retail dealers	20,390
Laborers in public service	29,591
Soldiers, sailors	12,511
Clergymen	19,343

Barbers, etc.	18,692
Janitors	38,662
Porters not in stores	59,197
Servants	80,209
Waiters	31,681
Clerks except in stores	14,014
Messengers	12,587

Females

Farmers	79,893
Farm laborers	527,937
Dressmakers and seamstresses	26,961
Semi-skilled operatives in cigar and tobacco factories	13,446
Teachers	29,244
Hairdressers and manicurists	12,660
Housekeepers and stewards	13,250
Laundresses not in laundries	283,557
Laundry operatives	21,084
Midwives and nurses (not trained)	13,888
Servants	401,381
Waiters	14,155

This has been the gift of labor, one of the greatest that the Negro has made to American nationality. It was in part involuntary, but whether given willingly or not, it was given and America profited by the gift. This labor was always of the highest economic and even spiritual importance. During the World War for instance, the most important single thing that America could do for the Allies was to furnish them with materials. The actual fighting of American troops, while important, was not nearly as important as American food and munitions; but this material must not only be supplied, it must be transported, handled and delivered in America and in France; and it was here that the Negro stevedore troops behind the battle line—men who received no medals and little mention and were in fact despised as all manual workers have always been despised,—it was these men that made the victory of the Allies certain by their desperately difficult but splendid work. The first colored stevedores went over in June, 1917, and were followed by about 50,000 volunteers. To these were added later nearly 200,000 drafted men.

To all this we must add the peculiar spiritual contribution which the Negro made to Labor. Always physical fact has its spiritual complement, but in this case the gift is apt to be forgotten or slurred over. This gift is the thing that is usually known as "laziness". Again and again men speak of the laziness of Negro labor and some suppose that slavery of Negroes was necessary on that account; and that even in freedom Negroes must be "driven". On the other hand and in contradiction to this is the fact that Negroes do work and work efficiently. In South Africa and in Nigeria, in the Sudan and in Brazil, in the West Indies and all over the United States Negro labor has accomplished tremendous tasks. One of its latest and greatest tasks has been the building of the Panama Canal. These two sets of facts, therefore, would seem to be mutually contradictory, and many a northern manager has seen the contradiction when, facing the apparent laziness of Negro hands, he has attempted to drive them and found out that he could not and at the same time has afterward seen someone used to Negro labor get a tremendous amount of work out of the same gangs. The explanation of all this is clear and simple: The Negro laborer has not been trained in modern organized industry but rather in quite a different school.

The European workman works long hours and every day in the week because it is only in this way that he can support himself and family. With the present organization of industry and methods of distributing the results of industry any failure of the European workingman to toil hard and steadily would mean either starvation or social disgrace through the lowering of his standard of living. The Negro workingman on the other hand came out of an organization of industry which was communistic and did not call for unlimited toil on the part of the workers. There was work and hard work to do, for even in the fertile tropical lands the task of fighting weeds, floods, animals, insects and germs was no easy thing. But on the other hand the distribution of products was much simpler and fairer and the wants of the people were less developed. The black tropical worker therefore looked upon work as a necessary evil and maintained his right to balance the relative allurements of leisure and satisfaction at any particular day, hour or season. Moreover in the simple work-organization of tropical or semi-tropical life individual desires of this sort did not usually disarrange the whole economic process or machine.[16]

---

16. Olivier, *White Capital and Coloured Labor,* Chapter 8, London, 1906.

The white laborer therefore brought to America the habit of regular, continuous toil which he regarded as a great moral duty. The black laborer brought the idea of toil as a necessary evil ministering to the pleasure of life. While the gift of the white laborer made America rich, or at least made many Americans rich, it will take the psychology of the black man to make it happy. New and better organization of industry and a clearer conception of the value of effort and a wider knowledge of the process of production must come in, so as to increase the wage of the worker and decrease rent, interest, and profit; and then the black laborer's subconscious contribution to current economics will be recognized as of tremendous and increasing importance.

III

BLACK SOLDIERS

How the Negro fought in every American war for a cause that was not his and to gain for others a freedom which was not his own.

1. Colonial Wars

THE DAY IS PAST WHEN historians glory in war. Rather, with all thoughtful men, they deplore the barbarism of mankind which has made war so large a part of human history. As long, however, as there are powerful men who are determined to have their way by brute force, and as long as these men can compel or persuade enough of their group, nation or race to support them even to the limit of destruction, rape, theft and murder, just so long these men will and must be opposed by force—moral force if possible, physical force in the extreme. The world has undoubtedly come to the place where it defends reluctantly such defensive war, but has no words of excuse for offensive war, for the initiation of the program of physical force.

There is, however, one further consideration: the man in the ranks has usually little chance to decide whether the war is defensive or offensive, righteous or wrong. He is called upon to put life and limb in jeopardy. He responds, sometimes willingly with uplifted soul and high resolve, persuaded that he is under Divine command; sometimes by compulsion and by the iron of discipline. In all cases he has by every nation been given credit; and certainly the man who voluntarily lays down his life for a cause which he has been led to believe is righteous deserves public esteem, although the world may weep at his ignorance and blindness.

From the beginning America was involved in war because it was born in a day of war. First, there were wars, mostly of aggression but partly of self-defense, against the Indians. Then there was a series of wars which were but colonial echoes of European brawls. Next the United States fought to make itself independent of the economic suzerainty of England. After that came the conquest of Mexico and the war for the Union which resolved itself in a war against slavery, and finally the Spanish War and the great World War.

In all these wars the Negro has taken part. He cannot be blamed for them so far as they were unrighteous wars (and some of them were unrighteous), because he was not a leader: he was for the most part a common soldier in the ranks and did what he was told. Yet in the majority of cases he was not compelled to fight. He used his own judgment and he fought because he believed that by fighting for America he would gain the respect of the land and personal and spiritual freedom. His problem as a soldier was always peculiar: no matter for what America fought and no matter for what her enemies fought, the American Negro always fought for his own freedom and for the self-respect of his race. Whatever the cause of war, therefore, his cause was peculiarly just. He appears, therefore, in American wars always with double motive,—the desire to oppose the so-called enemy of his country along with his fellow white citizens, and before that, the motive of deserving well of those citizens and securing justice for his folk. In this way he appears in the earliest times fighting with the whites against the Indians as well as with the Indians against the whites, and throughout the history of the West Indies and Central America as well as the Southern United States we find here and there groups of Negroes fighting with the whites. For instance: in Louisiana early in the eighteenth century when Governor Perier took office, the colony was very much afraid of a combination between the Choctaw Indians and the fierce Banbara Negroes who had begun to make common cause with them. To offset this, Perier armed a band of slaves in 1729 and sent them against the Indians. He says: "The Negroes executed their mission with as much promptitude as secrecy." Later, in 1730, the Governor sent twenty white men and six Negroes to carry ammunition to the Illinois settlement up the Mississippi River. Perier says fifteen Negroes "in whose hands we had put weapons performed prodigies of valor. If the blacks did not cost so much and if their labor was not so necessary to the colony it would be better to turn them into soldiers and to dismiss those we have who are so bad and so cowardly that they seem to have been manufactured purposely for this colony." But this policy of using the Negroes against the Indians led the Indians to retaliate and seek alliance with the blacks and in August 1730, the Natchez Indians and the Chickshaws conspired with the Negroes to revolt. The head of the revolt, Samba, with eight of his confederates was executed before the conspiracy came to a head. In 1733, when Governor Bienville returned to power, he had an army consisting of 544 white men and 45 Negroes, the latter with free black officers.[1]

In the colonial wars which distracted America during the seventeenth and early part of the eighteenth centuries the Negro took comparatively small part because the institution of slavery was becoming more settled and the masters were afraid to let their slaves fight. Notwithstanding this, there were black freedmen who voted and were enrolled in the militia and went to war, while some masters sent their slaves as laborers and servants. As early as 1652 a law of Massachusetts as to the militia required "Negro, Scotchmen and Indians" to enroll in the militia. Afterward the policy was changed and Negroes and Indians were excluded but Negroes often acted as sentinels at meeting-house doors. At other times slaves ran away and enlisted as soldiers or as sailors, thus often gaining their liberty. The New York *Gazette* in 1760 advertises for a slave who is suspected of having enlisted "in the provincial service." In 1763 the Boston *Evening Post* was looking for a Negro who "was a soldier last summer." One mulatto in 1746 is advertised for in the Pennsylvania *Gazette*. He had threatened to go to the French and Indians and fight for them. And in the Maryland *Gazette*, 1755, gentlemen are warned that their slaves may run away to the French and Indians.[2]

2. The Revolutionary War

THE ESTIMATES OF THE NEGRO soldiers who fought on the American side of the Revolutionary War vary from four to six thousand, or one out of every 50 or 60 of the colonial troops.

On August 24, 1778, the following report was made of Negroes in the Revolutionary Army:[3]

Brigades	Present	Sick Absent	On Command	Total
North Carolina	42	10	6	58
Woodford	36	3	1	40
Muhlenburg.	64	26	8	98
Smallwood.	20	3	1	24

1. Alice Dunbar Nelson, *Journal of Negro History,* Vol. 1, pp. 369, 370, 371.
2. Cf. Livermore, *Opinion of the Founders of the Republic,* etc., part 2; *Journal of Negro History,* Vol. 1, p. 198ff.
3. G. H. Moore, *Historical Notes,* etc., N. Y., 1862.

2nd Maryland	43	15	2	60
Wayne	2			2
2nd Pennsylvania.	33	1	1	35
Clinton	33	2	4	62
Parsons	117	12	19	148
Huntington	56	2	4	62
Nixon.	26		1	27
Paterson.	64	13	12	89
Late Learned.	34	4	8	46
Poor.	16	7	4	27
Total.	586	98	71	755

Alex. Scammell, *Adj. Gen.*

This report does not include Negro soldiers enlisted in Rhode Island, Connecticut, New York, New Hampshire and other States not mentioned nor does it include those who were in the army at both earlier and later dates. Other records prove that Negroes served in as many as 18 brigades.

It was a Negro who in a sense began the actual fighting. In 1750 William Brown of Framingham, Mass., advertised three times for "A Molatto Fellow about 27 Years of Age, named *Crispas,* 6 Feet 2 Inches high, short Curl'd Hair." This runaway slave was the same Crispus Attucks who in 1779 led a mob on the 5th of March against the British soldiers in the celebrated "Boston Massacre."

Much has been said about the importance and lack of importance of this so-called "Boston Massacre." Whatever the verdict of history may be, there is no doubt that the incident loomed large in the eyes of the colonists. Distinguished men were orators on the 5th of March for years after, until that date was succeeded by the 4th of July. Daniel Webster in his great Bunker Hill oration said: "From that moment we may date the severance of the British Empire."

Possibly these men exaggerated the actual importance of a street brawl between citizens and soldiers, led by a runaway slave; but there is no doubt that the colonists, who fought for independence from England, thought this occasion of tremendous importance and were nerved to great effort because of it.

Livermore says: "The presence of the British soldiers in King Street excited the patriotic indignation of the people. The whole community was stirred, and sage counsellors were deliberating and writing and talking about the public grievances. But it was not for the 'wise and prudent' to be first to act against the encroachments of arbitrary power. 'A motley rabble of saucy boys, Negroes and mulattoes, Irish Teagues and outlandish Jack tars,' (as John Adams described them in his plea in defense of the soldiers) could not restrain their emotion or stop to enquire if what they *must do* was according to the letter of the law. Led by Crispus Attucks, the mulatto slave, and shouting, 'The way to get rid of these soldiers is to attack the main guard; strike at the root; this is the nest'; with more valor than discretion they rushed to King Street and were fired upon by Captain Preston's company. Crispus Attucks was the first to fall; he and Samuel Gray and Jonas Caldwell were killed on the spot. Samuel Maverick and Patrick Carr were mortally wounded. The excitement which followed was intense. The bells of the town were rung. An impromptu town meeting was held and an immense assembly gathered. Three days after, on the 8th, a public funeral of the Martyrs took place. The shops in Boston were closed and all the bells of Boston and the neighboring towns were rung. It is said that a greater number of persons assembled on this occasion than ever before gathered on this continent for a similar purpose. The body of Crispus Attucks, the mulatto, had been placed in Faneuil Hall with that of Caldwell, both being strangers in the city. Maverick was buried from his mother's house in Union Street, and Gray from his brother's in Royal Exchange Lane. The four hearses formed a junction in King Street and then the procession marched in columns six deep, with a long file of coaches belonging to the most distinguished citizens, to the Middle Burying Ground, where the four victims were deposited in one grave over which a stone was placed with the inscription:

> 'Long as in Freedom's cause the wise contend,
> Dear to your country shall your fame extend;
> While to the world the lettered stone shall tell
> Where Caldwell, Attucks, Gray and Maverick fell.'"

"The anniversary of this event was publicly commemorated in Boston by an oration and other exercises every year until our National Independence was achieved, when the Fourth of July was substituted for the Fifth of March as the more proper day for a general celebration.

Not only was the event commemorated but the martyrs who then gave up their lives were remembered and honored."[4]

The relation of the Negro to the Revolutionary War was peculiar. If his services were used by the Colonists this would be an excuse for the English to use the Indians and to emancipate the slaves. If he were not used not only was this source of strength to the small loyal armies neglected but there still remained the danger that the English would bid for the services of Negroes. At first then the free Negro went quite naturally into the army as he had for the most part been recognized as liable to military service. Then Congress hesitated and ordered that no Negroes be enlisted. Immediately there appeared the determination of the Negroes, whether deliberately arrived at or by the more or less unconscious development of thought under the circumstances, to give their services to the side which promised them freedom and decent treatment. When therefore Governor Dunmore of Virginia and English generals like Cornwallis and Clinton made a bid for the services of Negroes, coupled with promises of freedom, they got considerable numbers and in the case of Dunmore one Negro unit fought a pitched battle against the Colonists.

The Continental Congress took up the question of Negroes in the Army in September, 1775. A committee consisting of Lynch, Lee and Adams reported a letter which they had drafted to Washington. Rutledge of South Carolina moved that Washington be instructed to discharge all Negroes whether slave or free from the army, but this was defeated. October 8th Washington and other generals in council of war, agreed unanimously that slaves should be rejected and a large majority declared that they refuse free Negroes. October 18th, the question came up again before the committee consisting of Benjamin Franklin, General Washington, certain deputies, governors and others. This council agreed that Negroes should be rejected and Washington issued orders to this effect November 12th, 1775. Meantime, however, Dunmore's proclamation came and his later success in raising a black regiment which greatly disturbed Washington. In July, 1776, the British had 200 Negro soldiers on Long Island and later two regiments of Negroes were raised by the British in North Carolina. The South lost thousands of Negroes through the British. In Georgia a corps of fugitives calling themselves the "King of England Soldiers" kept

---

4. Livermore, pp. 115–16.

attacking on both sides of the Savannah River even after the Revolution and many feared a general insurrection of slaves.

The colonists soon began to change their attitude. Late in 1775, Washington reversed his decision and ordered his recruiting officers to accept free Negroes who had already served in the army and laid the matter before the Continental Congress. The Committee recommended that these Negroes be reenlisted but no others. Various leaders advised that it would be better to enlist the slaves, among them Samuel Hopkins, Alexander Hamilton, General Greene, James Madison. Even John Laurens of South Carolina tried to make the South accept the proposition.[5]

Thus Negroes again were received into the American army and from that time on they played important rôles. They had already distinguished themselves in individual cases at Bunker Hill. For instance, fourteen white officers sent the following statement to the Massachusetts Legislature on December 5, 1775: "The subscribers beg leave to report to your Honorable House (which we do in justice to the character of so brave a man) that under our own observation we declare that a Negro man named Salem Poor, of Colonel Frye's regiment, Captain Ames' company, in the late battle at Charlestown, behaved like an experienced officer as well as an excellent soldier. To set forth particulars of his conduct would be tedious. We only beg leave to say, in the person of this said Negro, centers a brave and gallant soldier. The reward due to so great and distinguished a character we submit to the Congress."[6]

They afterward fought desperately in Long Island and at the battle of Monmouth. Foreign travellers continually note the presence of Negroes in the American army.

Less known however is the help which the black republic of Haiti offered to the struggling Colonists. In December 1778 Savannah was captured by the British, and Americans were in despair until the French fleet appeared on the coast of Georgia in September 1779. The fleet offered to help recapture Savannah. It had on board 1900 French troops of whom 800 were black Haitian volunteers. Among these volunteers were Christophe, afterward king of Haiti, Rigaud, André, Lambert and others. They were a significant and faithful band which began by helping freedom in America, then turned and through the French revolution

---

5. Cf. Livermore and Moore as above; also *Journal of Negro History*, Vol. 1, pp. 114–20.
6. Livermore, p. 122. See also the account of Peter Salem, *do.*, pp. 118–21.

freed Haiti and finally helped in the emancipation of South America. The French troops landed below the city with the Americans at their right and together they made an attack. American and French flags were planted on the British outposts but their bearers were killed and a general retreat was finally ordered. Seven hundred and sixty Frenchmen and 312 Americans were killed and wounded. As the army began to retreat the British general attacked the rear, determined to annihilate the Americans. It was then that the black and mulatto freedmen from Haiti under the command of Viscount de Fontages made the charge on the English and saved the retreating Americans. They returned to Haiti to prepare eventually to make that country the second one in America which threw off the domination of Europe.[7]

Some idea of the number of Negro soldiers can be had by reference to documents mentioning the action of the States. Rhode Island raised a regiment of slaves, and Governor Cooke said that it was generally thought that at least 300 would enlist. Four companies were finally formed there at a cost of over £10,000. Most of the 629 slaves in New Hampshire enlisted and many of the 15,000 slaves in New York. Connecticut had Negroes in her regiments and also a regiment of colored soldiers. Maryland sought in 1781 to raise 750 Negro troops. Massachusetts had colored troops in her various units from 72 towns in that State. "In view of these numerous facts it is safe to conclude that there were at least 4,000 Negro soldiers scattered throughout the Continental Army."[8]

In a debate in Congress in 1820 two men, one from the North and one from the South, gave the verdict of that time on the value of the Negro in the Revolutionary War. William Eustis of Massachusetts said: "The war over and peace restored, these men returned to their respective States, and who could have said to them on their return to civil life after having shed their blood in common with the whites in the defense of the liberties of the country, 'You are not to participate in the rights secured by the struggle or in the liberty for which you have been fighting?' Certainly no white man in Massachusetts."

Charles Pinckney of South Carolina said: that the Negroes, "then were, as they still are, as valuable a part of our population to the Union as any other equal number of inhabitants. They were in numerous

7. T. G. Steward, in *Publications American Negro Academy*, No. 5, p. 12.
8. W. B. Hartgrove, *Journal of Negro History*, Vol. 1, pp. 125–9.

instances the pioneers and, in all, the laborers of your armies. To their hands were owing the erection of the greatest part of the fortifications raised for the protection of our country; some of which, particularly Fort Moultrie, gave at that early period of the inexperience and untried valor of our citizens, immortality to American arms: and, in the Northern States numerous bodies of them were enrolled into and fought by the sides of the whites, the battles of the Revolution."[9]

In 1779 in the war between Spain and Great Britain, the Spanish Governor of Louisiana, Galvez, had in his army which he led against the British, numbers of blacks and mulattoes who he said "behaved on all occasions with as much valor and generosity as the whites."[10]

3. The War of 1812

IN THE WAR OF 1812 the Negro appeared not only as soldier but particularly as sailor and in the dispute concerning the impressment of American sailors which was one of the causes of the war, Negro sailors repeatedly figured as seized by England and claimed as American citizens by America for whose rights the nation was apparently ready to go to war. For instance, on the Chesapeake were three Negro sailors whom the British claimed but whom the Americans declared were American citizens,—Ware, Martin and Strachen. As Bryant says: "The citizenship of Negroes was sought and defended by England and America at this time but a little later it was denied by the United States Supreme Court that Negroes could be citizens." On demand two of these Negroes were returned to America by the British government; the other one died in England.

Negroes fought under Perry and Macdonough. On the high seas Negroes were fighting. Nathaniel Shaler, captain of a privateer, wrote to his agent in New York in 1813:

"Before I could get our light sails on and almost before I could turn around, I was under the guns, not of a transport but of a large frigate! And not more than a quarter of a mile from her. . . Her first broadside killed two men and wounded six others. . . My officers conducted themselves in a way that would have done honor to a more permanent

---

9. Wilson, *Black Phalanx*, p. 71.
10. *Journal of Negro History,* Vol. 1, pp. 373–4; Gayarre's *History of Louisiana,* Vol. 3, p. 108.

service. . . The name of one of my poor fellows who was killed ought to be registered in the book of fame, and remembered with reverence as long as bravery is considered a virtue. He was a black man by the name of John Johnson. . . When America has such tars, she has little to fear from the tyrants of the ocean."[11]

A few Negroes were in the northern armies. A Congressman said in 1828: "I myself saw a battalion of them—as fine martial looking men as I ever saw attached to the northern army in the last war (1812) on its march from Plattsburg to Sacketts Harbor where they did service for the country with credit to New York and honor to themselves."[12]

But it was in the South that they furnished the most spectacular instance of participation in this war. Governor Claiborne appealed to General Jackson to use colored soldiers. "These men, Sir, for the most part, sustain good characters. Many of them have extensive connections and much property to defend, and all seem attached to arms. The mode of acting toward them at the present crisis, is an inquiry of importance. If we give them not our confidence, the enemy will be encouraged to intrigue and corrupt them."[13]

September 21, 1814, Jackson issued a spirited appeal to the free Negroes of Louisiana: "Through a mistaken policy, you have heretofore been deprived of a participation in the glorious struggle for national rights in which our country is engaged. This no longer shall exist."

"As sons of freedom, you are now called upon to defend our most inestimable blessing. As Americans, your country looks with confidence to her adopted children for a valorous support as a faithful return for the advantages enjoyed under her mild and equitable government. As fathers, husbands and brothers, you are summoned to rally around the standard of the Eagle, to defend all which is dear in existence. . . In the sincerity of a soldier and the language of truth I address you."[14]

He promised them the same bounty as whites and they were to have colored non-commissioned officers. There was some attempt to have Jackson tone down this appeal and say less of "equality," but he refused to change his first draft.

The news of this proclamation created great surprise in the North but not much criticism. Indeed, things were going too badly for the

11. Niles' *Register*, Feb. 26, 1814.

12. Wilson, *Black Phalanx*, p. 88.

13. Alice Dunbar-Nelson in *Journal of Negro History*, Vol. 2, p. 58.

14. Niles' Register, Vol. 7, p. 205.

Americans. The Capitol at Washington had been burned, the State of Maine was in British hands, enlistment had stopped and Northern States like New York were already arming Negroes. The Louisiana legislature, a month after Jackson's proclamation, passed an act authorizing two regiments of "men of color" by voluntary enlistment. Slaves were allowed to enlist and were publicly manumitted for their services. There were 3200 white and 430 colored soldiers in the battle of New Orleans. The first battalion of 280 Negroes was commanded by a white planter, La Coste; a second battalion of 150 was raised by Captain J. B. Savary, a colored man, from the San Dominican refugees, and commanded by Major Daquin who was probably a quadroon.

Besides these soldiers slaves were used in throwing up the famous cotton bale ramparts, which saved the city, and this was the idea of a black slave from Africa, who had seen the same thing done at home. Colored men were used to reconnoitre, and the slave trader Lafitte brought a mixed band of white and black fighters to help. Curiously enough there were also Negroes on the other side, Great Britain having imported a regiment from the West Indies which was at the head of the attacking column moving against Jackson's right, together with an Irish regiment. Conceive this astounding anomaly!

The American Negro soldiers were stationed very near Jackson and his staff. Jackson himself in an address to the soldiers after the battle, complimenting the "embodied militia," said:

"To the Men of Color.—Soldiers! From the shores of Mobile I collected you to arms,—I invited you to share in the perils and to divide the glory of your white countrymen. I expected much from you; for I was not uninformed of those qualities which must render you so formidable to an invading foe. I knew that you could endure hunger and thirst and all the hardships of war. I knew that you loved the land of your nativity and that, like ourselves, you had to defend all that is most dear to man. But you surpass my hopes. I have found in you, united to these qualities, that noble enthusiasm which impels to great deeds."[15]

In the celebration of the victory which followed in the great public square, the Place d'Armes, now Jackson Square, the colored troops shared the glory and the wounded prisoners were met by colored nurses.[16]

---

15. Niles' Register, Vol. 7, pp. 345–6.
16. Dunbar-Nelson in *Journal of Negro History*, Vol. 2, pp. 59–60.

4. The Civil War

THERE WERE A FEW NEGROES in the Mexican War but they went mostly as body servants to white officers and there were probably no soldiers and certainly no distinct Negro organizations. The Negro, therefore, shares little of the blood guilt of that unhallowed raid for slave soil.

At the time of the Civil War when the call came for volunteers free Negroes everywhere offered their services to the Northern States and everywhere their services were declined. Indeed, it was almost looked upon as insolence that they should offer to fight in this "white man's war." Not only was the war to be fought by white men but desperate effort was made to cling to the technical fact that this was a war to save the Union and not a war against slavery. Federal officials and northern army officers made effort to reassure the South that they were not abolitionists and that they were not going to touch slavery.[17]

Meantime there began to crystallize the demand that the real object of the war be made the abolition of slavery and that the slaves and colored men in general be allowed to fight for freedom.

This met bitter opposition. The New York *Herald* voiced this August 5, 1862. "The efforts of those who love the Negro more than the Union to induce the President to swerve from his established policy are unavailing. He will neither be persuaded by promises nor intimidated by threats. Today he was called upon by two United States Senators and rather peremptorily requested to accept the services of two Negro regiments. They were flatly and unequivocally rejected. The President did not appreciate the necessity of employing the Negroes to fight the battles of the country and take the positions which the white men of the nation, the voters, and sons of patriotic sires, should be proud to occupy; there were employments in which the Negroes of rebel masters might well be engaged, but he was not willing to place them upon an equality with our volunteers who had left home and family and lucrative occupations to defend the Union and the Constitution while there were volunteers or militia enough in the loyal States to maintain the Government without resort to this expedient. If the loyal people were not satisfied with the policy he had adopted, he was willing to leave the administration to other hands. One of the

---

17. Williams, *Negro Race in America*, Vol. 2, pp. 244ff.

Senators was impudent enough to tell the President he wished to God he would resign."

In the spring of 1862 General Hunter was sent into South Carolina with less than 11,000 men and charged with the duty of holding the whole seacoast of Georgia, South Carolina and Florida. He asked for re-enforcement but was told frankly from Washington, "Not a man from the North can be spared." The only way to guard the position was to keep long lines of entrenchment thrown up against the enemy. General Hunter calmly announced his intention of forming a Negro regiment to help him. They were to be paid as laborers by the quartermaster but he expected eventually to have them recognized as soldiers by the government. At first he could find no officers. They were shocked at being asked to command "niggers." Even non-commissioned officers were difficult to find. But eventually the regiment was formed and became an object of great curiosity when on parade. Reports of the first South Carolina infantry were sent to Washington but there was no reply. Then suddenly the matter came up in Congress and Hunter was ordered to explain whether he had enlisted fugitive slaves and upon what authority. Hunter immediately sent a sharp reply:

"To the first question, therefore, I reply: That no regiment of 'fugitive slaves' has been, or is being, organized in this department. There is, however, a fine regiment of loyal persons whose late masters are fugitive rebels—men who everywhere fly before the appearance of the National flag, leaving their loyal and unhappy servants behind them, to shift as best they can for themselves. So far, indeed, are the loyal persons composing the regiment from seeking to evade the presence of their late owners, that they are now one and all endeavoring with commendable zeal to acquire the drill and discipline requisite to place them in a position to go in full and effective pursuit of their fugacious and traitorous proprietors.

"The experiment of arming the blacks, so far as I have made it, has been a complete and even marvellous success. They are sober, docile, attentive and enthusiastic, displaying great natural capacities in acquiring the duties of the soldier. They are now eager beyond all things to take the field and be led into action; and it is the unanimous opinion of the officers who have had charge of them, that in the peculiarities of this climate and country, they will prove invaluable auxiliaries, fully equal to the similar regiments so long and so successfully used by the British authorities in the West India Islands.

"In conclusion, I would say, it is my hope—there appearing no possibility of other re-inforcements, owing to the exigencies of the campaign in the peninsula—to have organized by the end of next fall and to be able to present to the government from 48,000 to 50,000 of these hardy and devoted soldiers."[18]

The reply was read in Congress amid laughter despite the indignation of the Kentucky Congressman who instituted the inquiry.

Protests now came from the South but no answer was forthcoming and despite all the agitation the regiment remained until at last Hunter was officially ordered to raise 50,000 black laborers of whom 5,000 might be armed and dressed as soldiers.

Horace Greeley stated the case clearly August 20, 1862 in his "Prayer of Twenty Million":[19]

"On the face of this wide earth, Mr. President, there is not one disinterested, determined, intelligent champion of the Union cause who does not feel that all attempts to put down the rebellion and at the same time uphold its inciting cause are preposterous and futile—that the rebellion if crushed out tomorrow would be renewed within a year if slavery were left in full vigor—that army officers who remain to this day devoted to slavery can at best be but half-way loyal to the Union—and that every hour of deference to slavery is an hour of added and deepened peril to the Union. . .

"I close as I began, with the statement that what an immense majority of the loyal millions of your countrymen require of you is a frank, declared, unqualified, ungrudging execution of the laws of the land, more especially of the Confiscation Act. That Act gives freedom to the slaves of rebels coming within our lines or whom those lines may at any time enclose,—we ask you to render it due obedience by publicly requiring all your subordinates to recognize and obey it. The rebels are everywhere using the late anti-Negro riots in the North—as they have long used your officers' treatment of Negroes in the South— to convince the slaves that they have nothing to hope from a Union success—that we mean in that case to sell them into bitter bondage to defray the cost of the war. Let them impress this as a truth on the great mass of their ignorant and credulous bondsmen, and the Union will never be restored—never. We cannot conquer ten millions of

18. Williams, *Negro Race in America*, Vol. 2, pp. 280–82.
19. New York *Tribune*, Aug. 19, 1862.

W.E.B. DU BOIS

people united in solid phalanx against us, powerfully aided by northern sympathizers and European allies. We must have scouts, guides, spies, cooks, teamsters, diggers and choppers from the blacks of the South—whether we allow them to fight for us or not—or we shall be baffled and repelled."

A month later, September 22, Abraham Lincoln issued the preliminary Emancipation Proclamation. He had considered this step before and his final decision was caused, first, by a growing realization of the immense task that lay before the Union armies and, secondly, by the fear that Europe was going to recognize the Confederacy, since she saw as between North and South little difference in attitude toward slavery.

The effect of the step was undoubtedly decisive for ultimate victory, although at first it spread dismay. Six of the Northern States went Democratic in the fall elections and elsewhere the Republicans lost heavily. In the army some officers resigned and others threatened to because "The war for the Union was changed into a war for the Negro."

In the South men like Beauregard urged the raising of the "Black Flag" while Jefferson Davis in his third annual message wrote: "We may well leave it to the instincts of that common humanity which a beneficent Creator has implanted in the breasts of our fellowmen of all countries to pass judgment on a measure by which several millions of human beings of an inferior race, peaceful and contented laborers in their sphere, are doomed to extermination."[20]

With emancipation foreshadowed the full recognition of the Negro soldier was inevitable. In September 1862 came a black Infantry Regiment From Louisiana and later a regiment of heavy artillery and by the end of 1862 four Negro regiments had enlisted. Immediately after the signing of the Emancipation Proclamation came the Kansas Colored volunteers and the famous 54th Massachusetts Regiment. A Bureau was established in Washington to handle the colored enlistments and before the end of the war 178,975 Negroes had enlisted.

"In the Department (of War) the actual number of Negroes enlisted was never known, from the fact that a practice prevailed of putting a live Negro in a dead one's place. For instance, if a company on picket or scouting lost ten men, the officer would immediately put ten new men in their places and have them answer to the dead men's names. I learn from very reliable sources that this was done in Virginia, also in Missouri and

---

20. Williams, Vol. 2, p. 271.

Tennessee. If the exact number of men could be ascertained, instead of 180,000 it would doubtless be in the neighborhood of 220,000 who entered the ranks of the army."[21]

General orders covering the enlistment of Negro troops were sent out from the War Department October 13, 1863. The Union League in New York city raised 2,000 black soldiers in 45 days, although no bounty was offered them and no protection promised their families. The regiment had a triumphal march through the city and a daily paper stated: "In the month of July last the homes of these people were burned and pillaged by an infuriated political mob; they and their families were hunted down and murdered in the public streets of this city; and the force and majesty of the law were powerless to protect them. Seven brief months have passed and a thousand of these despised and persecuted men marched through the city in the garb of the United States soldiers, in vindication of their own manhood and with the approval of a countless multitude—in effect saving from inevitable and distasteful conscription the same number of those who hunted their persons and destroyed their homes during those days of humiliation and disgrace. This is noble vengeance—a vengeance taught by Him who commanded, 'Love them that hate you; do good to them that persecute you.'"

The enlistment of Negroes caused difficulty and friction among the white troops. In South Carolina General Gilmore had to forbid the white troops using Negro troops for menial service in cleaning up the camps. Black soldiers in uniform often had their uniforms stripped off by white soldiers.

"I attempted to pass Jackson Square in New Orleans one day in my uniform when I was met by two white soldiers of the 24th Conn. They halted me and then ordered me to undress. I refused, when they seized me and began to tear my coat off. I resisted, but to no good purpose; a half dozen others came up and began to assist. I recognized a sergeant in the crowd, an old shipmate on board of a New Bedford, Mass., whaler; he came to my rescue, my clothing was restored and I was let go. It was nothing strange to see a black soldier *à la* Adam come into the barracks out of the streets."[22] This conduct led to the killing of a portion of a boat's crew of the U. S. Gunboat Jackson, at Ship Island, Miss., by members of a Negro regiment stationed there.

---

21. Wilson, p. 123.
22. Wilson, p. 132.

Then, too, there was contemptible discrimination in pay. While white soldiers received $13 a month and clothing, Negro soldiers, by act of Congress, were given $10 a month with $3 deducted for clothing, leaving only $7 a month as actual pay. This was only remedied when the 54th Massachusetts Infantry refused all pay for a year until it should be treated as other regiments. The State of Massachusetts made up the difference between the $7 and $13 to disabled soldiers until June 16, 1864, when the government finally made the Negroes' pay equal to that of the whites.

On the Confederate side there was a movement to use Negro soldiers fostered by Judah Benjamin, General Lee and others. In 1861 a Negro company from Nashville offered its services to the Confederate states and free Negroes of Memphis were authorized by the Committee of Safety to organize a volunteer company. Companies of free Negroes were raised in New Orleans,—"Very well drilled and comfortably uniformed." In Richmond colored troops were also raised in the last days. Few if any of these saw actual service. Plantation hands from Alabama built the redoubts at Charleston, and Negroes worked as teamsters and helpers throughout the South. In February, 1864, the Confederate congress provided for the impressment of 20,000 slaves for menial service, and President Davis suggested that the number be doubled and that they be emancipated at the end of their service. Before the war started local authorities had in many cases enrolled free Negroes as soldiers and some of these remained in the service of the Confederacy. The adjutant general of the Louisiana militia issued an order which said "the Governor and the Commander-in-Chief, relying implicitly upon the loyalty of the free colored population of the city and State, for the protection of their homes, their property and for southern rights, from the population of a ruthless invader, and believing that the military organization which existed prior to February 15, 1862, and elicited praise and respect for the patriotic motives which prompted it, should exist for and during the war, calls upon them to maintain their organization and hold themselves prepared for such orders as may be transmitted to them." These native guards did not leave the city when the Confederates did and explained to General Butler that they dared not refuse to work with the Confederates and that they hoped by their service to gain greater equality with the whites and that they would be glad now to join the Union forces. Two weeks after the fall of Sumter colored volunteers passed through Georgia on their way to Virginia.

There were 16 or more companies. In November, 1861, a regiment of 1,400 free colored men were in the line of march at New Orleans. The idea of calling the Negroes grew as the power of the Confederacy waned and the idea of emancipation as compensation spread. President Davis said "Should the alternative ever be presented of subjugation or of the employment of slaves as soldiers there seems no reason to doubt what should be our decision."

There was, of course, much difference of opinion. General Cobb said "If slaves make good soldiers our whole theory of slavery is wrong," while a Georgian replied "Some say that Negroes will not fight, I say they will fight. They fought at Ocean Pond, Honey Hill and other places." General Lee, in January '64, gave as his opinion that they should employ them without delay. "I believe with proper regulations they may be made efficient soldiers." He continued, "Our chief aim should be to secure their fidelity. There have been formidable armies composed of men having no interest in the cause for which they fought beyond their pay or the hope of plunder. But it is certain that the surest foundation upon which the fidelity of an army can rest, especially in a service which imposes hardships and privations, is the personal interest of the soldier in the issue of the contest. Such an interest we can give our Negroes by giving immediate freedom to all who enlist, and freedom at the end of the war to the families of those who discharge their duties faithfully (whether they survive or not), together with the privilege of residing at the South. To this might be added a bounty for faithful service."

Finally, March 13, 1865, it was directed that slaves be enrolled in the Confederate army, each state to furnish its quota of 300,000. Recruiting officers were appointed, but before the plan could be carried out Lee and Johnson surrendered.[23]

The central fact which we forget in these days is that the real question in the minds of most white people in the United States in 1863 was whether or not the Negro really would fight. The generation then living had never heard of the Negro in the Revolution and in the War of 1812, much less of his struggles and insurrections before. From 1820 down to the time of the war a determined and far-reaching propaganda had led most men to believe in the natural inferiority, cowardice and degradation of the Negro race. We have already seen Abraham Lincoln suggest that if arms were put into the hands of the Negro soldier it might be simply

---

23. Wesley, in *Journal of Negro History,* Vol. 4, pp. 239ff.

a method of arming the rebels. The New York *Times* discussed the matter soberly, defending the right to employ Negroes but suggesting four grounds which might make it inexpedient; that Negroes would not fight, that prejudice was so strong that whites would not fight with them, that no free Negroes would volunteer and that slaves could not be gotten hold of and that the use of Negroes would exasperate the South. "The very best thing that can be done under existing circumstances, in our judgment, is to possess our souls in patience while the experiment is being tried. The problem will probably speedily solve itself—much more speedily than heated discussion or harsh criminations can solve it."

This was in February 16, 1863. It was not long before the results of using Negro troops began to be reported and we find the *Times* saying editorially on the 31st of July: "Negro soldiers have now been in battle at Port Hudson and at Milliken's Bend in Louisiana; at Helena in Arkansas, at Morris Island in South Carolina, and at or near Fort Gibson in the Indian Territory. In two of these instances they assaulted fortified positions and led the assault; in two they fought on the defensive, and in one they attacked rebel infantry. In all of them they acted in conjunction with white troops and under command of white officers. In some instances they acted with distinguished bravery, and in all they acted as well as could be expected of raw troops."

On the 11th of February, 1863, the news columns of the *Times* were still more enthusiastic. "It will not need many such reports as this—and there have been several before it—to shake our inveterate Saxon prejudice against the capacity and courage of Negro troops. Everybody knows that they were used in the Revolution, and in the last war with Great Britain fought side by side with white troops, and won equal praises from Washington and Jackson. It is shown also that black sailors are on equal terms with their white comrades. If on the sea, why not on the land? No officer who has commanded black troops has yet reported against them. They are tried in the most unfavorable and difficult circumstances, but never fail. When shall we learn to use the full strength of the formidable ally who is only waiting for a summons to rally under the flag of the Union? Colonel Higginson says: 'No officer in this regiment now doubts that the successful prosecution of this war lies in the unlimited employment of black troops.' The remark is true in a military sense, and it has a still deeper political significance."

"When General Hunter has scattered 50,000 muskets among the Negroes of the Carolinas, and General Butler has organized the

100,000 or 200,000 blacks for whom he may perhaps shortly carry arms to New Orleans, the possibility of restoring the Union as it was, with slavery again its dormant power, will be seen to have finally passed away. The Negro is indeed the key to success."

The Negroes began to fight and fight hard: but their own and peculiar characteristics stood out even in the blood of war. A Pennsylvania Major wrote home: "I find that these colored men learn everything that pertains to the duties of a soldier much faster than any white soldiers I have ever seen. . . They are willing, obedient, and cheerful; move with agility, and are full of music."[24]

Certain battles, carnivals of blood, stand out and despite their horror must not be forgotten. One of the earliest encounters was the terrible massacre at Fort Pillow, April 18, 1863. The fort was held with a garrison of 557 men, of whom 262 were colored soldiers of the 6th United States Heavy Artillery. The Union commander refused to surrender.

"Upon receiving the refusal of Major Booth to capitulate, Forrest gave a signal and his troops made a frantic charge upon the fort. It was received gallantly and resisted stubbornly, but there was no use of fighting. In ten minutes the enemy, assaulting the fort in the centre, and striking it on the flanks, swept in. The Federal troops surrendered; but an indiscriminate massacre followed. Men were shot down in their tracks; pinioned to the ground with bayonet and sabre. Some were clubbed to death while dying of wounds; others were made to get down upon their knees, in which condition they were shot to death. Some were burned alive, having been fastened into the buildings, while still others were nailed against the houses, tortured and then burned to a crisp."[25]

May 27, 1863, came the battle of Port Hudson. "Hearing the firing apparently more fierce and continuous to the right than anywhere else, I turned in that direction, past the sugar house of Colonel Chambers, where I had slept, and advanced to near the pontoon bridge across the Big Sandy Bayou, which the Negro regiments had erected, and where they were fighting most desperately. I had seen these brave and hitherto despised fellows the day before as I rode along the lines, and I had seen General Banks acknowledge their respectful salute as he would have

24. New York *Tribune,* Nov. 14, 1863; Williams, Vol. 2, p. 347.
25. Williams, Vol. 2, p. 360.

done that of any white troops; but still the question was—with too many—'Will they fight?'

"General Dwight, at least, must have had the idea, not only that they were men, but something more than men, from the terrific test to which he put their valor. Before any impression had been made upon the earthworks of the enemy, and in full face of the batteries belching forth their 62-pounders, these devoted people rushed forward to encounter grape, canister, shell, and musketry, with no artillery but two small howitzers—that seemed mere popguns to their adversaries—and no reserve whatever.

"Their force consisted of the 1st Louisiana Native Guards (with colored field officers) under Lieutenant-Colonel Bassett, and the 3d Louisiana Native Guards, Colonel Nelson (with white field officers), the whole under command of the latter officer.

"On going into action they were 1,080 strong, and formed into four lines, Lieutenant-Colonel Bassett, 1st Louisiana, forming the first line, and Lieutenant-Colonel Henry Finnegas the second. When ordered to charge up the works, they did so with the skill and nerve of old veterans (black people, be it remembered who had never been in action before). Oh, but the fire from the rebel guns was so terrible upon the unprotected masses, that the first few shots mowed them down like grass and so continued.

"Colonel Bassett being driven back, Colonel Finnegas took his place, and his men being similarly cut to pieces, Lieutenant-Colonel Bassett reformed and recommenced; and thus these brave people went in from morning until 3:30 P.M., under the most hideous carnage that men ever had to withstand, and that very few white ones would have had nerve to encounter, even if ordered to.

"During this time, they rallied, and were ordered to make six distinct charges, losing 37 killed, and 155 wounded, and 116 missing,—the majority, if not all, of these being, in all probability, now lying dead on the gory field, and without the rites of sepulture; for when, by flag of truce, our forces in other directions were permitted to reclaim their dead, the benefit, through some neglect, was not extended to these black regiments.

"The deeds of heroism performed by these colored men were such as the proudest white men might emulate. Their colors are torn to pieces by shot and literally bespattered by blood and brains. The color-sergeant of the 1st Louisiana, on being mortally wounded, hugged the colors to his breast, when a struggle ensued between the two color-corporals on each side of him, as to who should have the honor of bearing the sacred standard, and during this generous contention one was seriously wounded. One black lieutenant actually mounted the enemy's works three or four times, and in one charge the assaulting party came within fifty paces of them. Indeed, if only ordinarily supported by artillery and reserve, no one can convince us that they would not have opened a passage through the enemy's works.

"Captain Callioux of the 1st Louisiana, a man so black that he actually prided himself upon his blackness, died the death of a hero, leading on his men in the thickest of the fight."[26]

In July 13, 1863, came the draft riot in New York when the daily papers told the people that they were called upon to fight the battles of "niggers and abolitionists," when the governor did nothing but "request" the rioters to await the report of his demand that the President suspend the draft. Meantime the city was given over to rapine and murder, property destroyed, Negroes killed and the colored orphans' asylum burned to the ground and property robbed and pillaged.

At that very time in South Carolina black soldiers were preparing to take Fort Wagner, their greatest battle. It will be noted that continually Negroes were called upon to rescue lost causes, many times as a sort of deliberate test of their courage. Fort Wagner was a case in point. The story may be told from two points of view, that of the white Unionist and that of the Confederate. The Union account says:

"The signal given, our forces advanced rapidly towards the fort, while our mortars in the rear tossed their bombs over their heads. The 54th Massachusetts (a Negro Regiment) led the attack, supported by the 6th Connecticut, 48th New York, 3rd New Hampshire, 76th Pennsylvania, and the 9th Maine Regiments. . . The silent and shattered walls of Wagner all at once burst forth into a blinding sheet of vivid light, as though they had suddenly been transformed by some magic power into the living, seething crater of a volcano! Down came the whirlwind of destruction along the beach with the swiftness of lightning! How fearfully the hissing shot, the shrieking bombs, the whistling bars of iron, and the whispering bullet struck and crushed through the dense masses of our brave men! I never shall forget the terrible sound of that awful blast of death, which swept down, shattered

---

26. New York *Times,* June 13, 1863.

or dead, a thousand of our men. Not a shot had missed its aim. Every bolt of steel, every globe of iron and lead, tasted of human blood. . .

"In a moment the column recovered itself, like a gallant ship at sea when buried for an instant under the immense wave.

"The ditch is reached; a thousand men leap into it, clamber up the shattered ramparts, and grapple with the foe, which yields and falls back to the rear of the fort. Our men swarm over the walls, bayoneting the desperate rebel cannoneers. Hurrah! the fort is ours!

"But now came another blinding blast from concealed guns in the rear of the fort, and our men went down by scores. . . The struggle is terrific. Our supports hurry up to the aid of their comrades, but as they reach the ramparts they fire a volley which strikes down many of our men. Fatal mistake! Our men rally once more; but, in spite of an heroic resistance, they are forced back again to the edge of the ditch. Here the brave Shaw, with scores of his black warriors, went down, fighting desperately."

When asking for the body of Colonel Shaw, a confederate major said: "We have buried him with his niggers."

The Confederate account is equally eloquent.

"The carnage was frightful. It is believed the Federals lost more men on that eventful night than twice the entire strength of the Confederate garrison. . . According to the statement of Chaplain Dennison the assaulting columns, in two brigades, commanded by General Strong and Colonel Putnam (the division under General Seymour), consisted of the 54th Massachusetts, 3rd and 7th New Hampshire, 6th Connecticut and 100th New York, with a reserve brigade commanded by General Stephenson. One of the assaulting regiments was composed of Negroes (the 54th Massachusetts) and to it was assigned the honor of leading the white columns to the charge. It was a dearly purchased compliment. Their Colonel (Shaw) was killed upon the parapet and the regiment almost annihilated, although the Confederates in the darkness could not tell the color of their assailants."[27]

At last it was seen that Negro troops could do more than useless or helpless or impossible tasks, and in the siege of Petersburg they were put to important work. When the general attack was ordered on the 16th of June, 1864, a division of black troops was used. The Secretary of War, Stanton himself, saw them and said:

---

27. Wilson, pp. 250–54.

"The hardest fighting was done by the black troops. The forts they stormed were the worst of all. After the affair was over General Smith went to thank them, and tell them he was proud of their courage and dash. He says they cannot be exceeded as soldiers, and that hereafter he will send them in a difficult place as readily as the best white troops."[28]

It was planned to send the colored troops under Burnside against the enemy after the great mine was exploded. Inspecting officers reported to Burnside that the black division was fitted for this perilous work. The white division which was sent made a fiasco of it. Then, after all had been lost Burnside was ready to send in his black division and though they charged again and again they were repulsed and the Union lost over 4,000 men killed, wounded and captured.

All the officers of the colored troops in the Civil War were not white. From the first there were many colored non-commissioned officers, and the Louisiana regiments raised under Butler had 66 colored officers, including one Major and 27 Captains, besides the full quota of non-commissioned colored officers. In the Massachusetts colored troops there were 10 commissioned Negro officers and 3 among the Kansas troop. Among these officers was a Lieutenant-Colonel Reed of North Carolina, who was killed in battle. In Kansas there was Captain H. F. Douglas, and in other United States' volunteer regiments were Major M. H. Delaney and Captain O. S. B. Wall; Dr. A. T. Augusta, surgeon, was brevetted Lieutenant-Colonel. The losses of Negro troops in the Civil War, killed, wounded and missing has been placed at 68,178.

Such was the service of the Negro in the Civil War. Men say that the nation gave them freedom, but the verdict of history is written on the Shaw monument at the head of Boston Common:

THE WHITE OFFICERS

Taking Life and Honor in their Hands—Cast their lot with Men of a Despised Race Unproved in War—and Risked Death as Inciters of a Servile Insurrection if Taken Prisoners, Besides Encountering all the Common Perils of Camp, March, and Battle.

---

28. Williams, Vol. 2, p. 338.

Volunteered when Disaster Clouded the Union Cause—Served without Pay for Eighteen Months till Given that of White Troops—Faced Threatened Enslavement if Captured—Were Brave in Action—Patient under Dangerous and Heavy Labors and Cheerful amid Hardships and Privations.

Together

They Gave to the Nation Undying Proof that Americans of African Descent Possess the Pride, Courage, and Devotion of the Patriot Soldier—One Hundred and Eighty Thousand Such Americans Enlisted Under the Union Flag in MDCCCLXIII-MDCCCLXV.

5. The War in Cuba

IN THE SPANISH-AMERICAN WAR FOUR Negro regiments were among the first to be ordered to the front. They were the regular army regiments, 24th and 25th Infantry, and the 9th and 10th Cavalry. President McKinley recommended that new regiments of regular army troops be formed among Negroes but Congress took no action. Colored troops with colored officers were formed as follows: The 3rd North Carolina, the 8th Illinois, the 9th Battalion, Ohio and the 23rd Kansas. Regiments known as the Immunes, being immune to Yellow fever, were formed with colored lieutenants and white captains and field officers, and called the 7th, 8th, 9th and 10th United States Volunteers. In addition to those there were the 6th Virginia with colored lieutenants and the 3rd Alabama with white officers. Indiana had two companies attached to the 8th Immunes. None of the Negro volunteer companies reached the front in time to take part in battle. The 8th Illinois formed a part of the Army of Occupation and was noted for its policing and cleaning up of Santiago. Colonel John R. Marshall, commanding the 8th Illinois, and Major Charles Young, a regular army commander, both colored, were in charge of the battalion.

The colored regular army regiments took a brilliant part in the war. The first regiment ordered to the front was the 24th Infantry. Negro soldiers were in the battles around Santiago. The Tenth Cavalry made an effective attack at Las Quasimas and at El Caney on July 1 they saved Roosevelt's Rough Riders from annihilation. The 24th Infantry volunteered in the Yellow fever epidemic and cleaned the camp in one day. *Review of Reviews* says: "One of the most gratifying incidents of the Spanish War has been the enthusiassm that the colored regiments of the regular army have aroused throughout the whole country. Their fighting at Santiago was magnificent. The Negro soldiers showed excellent discipline, the highest qualities of personal bravery, very superior physical endurance, unfailing good temper, and the most generous disposition toward all comrades-in-arms, whether white or black. Roosevelt's Rough Riders have come back singing the praises of the colored troops. There is not a dissenting voice in the chorus of praise. . . Men who can fight for their country as did these colored troops ought to have their full share of gratitude and honor."

6. Carrizal

IN 1916 THE UNITED STATES sent a punitive expedition under General Pershing into Mexico in pursuit of the Villa forces which had raided Columbus, New Mexico. Two Negro regiments, the 10th Cavalry and the 24th Infantry, were a part of his expedition. On June 21, Troop C and K of the 10th Cavalry were ambushed at Carrizal by some 700 Mexican soldiers. Although outnumbered almost ten to one, these black soldiers dismounted in the face of a withering machine-gun fire, deployed, charged the Mexicans and killed their commander.

This handful of men fought on until, of the three officers commanding them, two were killed and one was badly wounded. Seventeen of the men were killed and twenty-three were made prisoners. One of the many outstanding heroes of this memorable engagement was Peter Bigstaff, who fought to the last beside his commander, Lieutenant Adair. A Southern white man, with no love for blacks, wrote:

"The black trooper might have faltered and fled a dozen times, saving his own life and leaving Adair to fight alone. But it never seemed to occur to him. He was a comrade to the last blow. When Adair's broken revolver fell from his hand the black trooper pressed another into it, and together, shouting in defiance, they thinned the swooping circle of overwhelming odds before them.

"The black man fought in the deadly shambles side by side with the white man, following always, fighting always as his lieutenant fought.

"And finally, when Adair, literally shot to pieces, fell in his tracks, his last command to his black trooper was to leave him and save his life. Even then the heroic Negro paused in the midst of that Hell of carnage for a final service to his officer. Bearing a charmed life, he had fought his way out. He saw that Adair had fallen with his head in the water. With superb loyalty the black trooper turned and went back to the maelstrom of death, lifted the head of his superior, leaned him against a tree and left him there dead with dignity when it was impossible to serve any more.

"There is not a finer piece of soldierly devotion and heroic comradeship in the history of modern warfare than that of Henry Adair and the black trooper who fought by him at Carrizal."[29]

7. The World War

FINALLY WE COME TO THE World War the history of which is not yet written. At first and until the United States entered the war the Negro figured as a laborer and a great exodus took place from the South as we have already noted. Some effort was made to keep the Negro from the draft but finally he was called and although constituting less than a tenth of the population he furnished 13% of the soldiers called to the colors. The registry for the draft had insulting color discriminations and determined effort was made to confine Negroes to stevedore and labor regiments under white officers. Most of the Negro draftees were thus sent to the Service of Supplies where they were largely under illiterate whites and suffered greatly. Finally a camp for training Negro officers was established and nearly 700 Negroes commissioned, none of them, however, above the rank of captain; Charles Young, the highest ranking Negro graduate of West Point and one of the best officers in the army was kept from the front, because being already a colonel with a distinguished record he would surely have become a general if sent to France.

Two Negro divisions were planned, the 92nd and the 93rd. The 93rd was to be composed of the Negro National Guard regiments all of whom had some and one all Negro officers. The latter division was never organized as a complete division but four of its regiments were sent to France and encountered bitter discrimination from the Americans on account of their Negro officers. They were eventually brigaded with the

---

29. John Temple Graves in *Review of Reviews*.

French and saw some of the hardest fighting of the war in the final drive toward Sedan. They were cited in General Orders as follows by General Goybet:[30]

"In transmitting to you with legitimate pride the thanks and congratulations of the General Garnier Duplessis, allow me, my dear friends of all ranks, Americans and French, to thank you from the bottom of my heart as a chief and a soldier for the expression of gratitude for the glory which you have lent our good 157th Division. I had full confidence in you but you have surpassed my hopes.

"During these nine days of hard fighting you have progressed nine kilometers through powerful organized defenses, taken nearly 600 prisoners, 15 guns of different calibers, 20 minnewerfers, and nearly 150 machine guns, secured an enormous amount of engineering material, an important supply of artillery ammunition, brought down by your fire three enemy aeroplanes.

"Your troops have been admirable in their attack. You must be proud of the courage of your officers and men; and I consider it an honor to have them under my command.

"The bravery and dash of your regiment won the admiration of the 2nd Moroccan Division who are themselves versed in warfare. Thanks to you, during those hard days, the Division was at all times in advance of all other divisions of the Army Corps. I am sending you all my thanks and beg you to transmit them to your subordinates.

"I called on your wounded. Their morale is higher than any praise.

GOYBET

The 92nd Division encountered difficulties in organization and was never assembled as a Division until it arrived in France. There it was finally gotten in shape and took a small part in the Argonne offensive and in the fight just preceding the armistice. Their Commanding General said:[31]

"Five months ago today the 92nd Division landed in France.

---

30. MS. Copies of orders.
31. MS. Copies of orders.

"After seven weeks of training, it took over a sector in the front line, and since that time some portion of the Division has been practically continuously under fire.

"It participated in the last battle of the war with creditable success, continuously pressing the attack against highly organized defensive works. It advanced successfully on the first day of the battle, attaining its objectives and capturing prisoners. This in the face of determined opposition by an alert enemy, and against rifle, machine-gun and artillery fire. The issue of the second day's battle was rendered indecisive by the order to cease firing at eleven A.M.—when the armistice became effective."

With the small chance thus afforded Negro troops nevertheless made a splendid record and especially those under Negro officers. If they had had larger opportunity and less organized prejudice they would have done much more. Perhaps their greatest credit is from the fact that they withstood so bravely and uncomplainingly the barrage of hatred and offensive prejudice aimed against them. The young Negro officers especially made a splendid record as to thinking, guiding leaders of an oppressed group.

Thus has the black man defended America from the beginning to the World War. To him our independence from Europe and slavery is in no small degree due.

IV

THE EMANCIPATION OF DEMOCRACY

How the black slave by his incessant struggle to be free has broadened the basis of democracy in America and in the world.

Help in exploration, labor unskilled and to some extent skilled; and fighting, have been the three gifts which so far we have considered as having been contributed by black folk to America. We now turn to a matter more indefinite and yet perhaps of greater importance.

Without the active participation of the Negro in the Civil War, the Union could not have been saved nor slavery destroyed in the nineteenth century.[1] Without the help of black soldiers, the independence of the United States could not have been gained in the eighteenth century. But the Negro's contribution to America was at once more subtle and important than these things. Dramatically the Negro is the central thread of American history. The whole story turns on him whether we think of the dark and flying slave ship in the sixteenth century, the expanding plantations of the seventeenth, the swelling commerce of the eighteenth, or the fight for freedom in the nineteenth. It was the black man that raised a vision of democracy in America such as neither Americans nor Europeans conceived in the eighteenth century and such as they have not even accepted in the twentieth century; and yet a conception which every clear sighted man knows is true and inevitable.

1. Democracy

DEMOCRACY WAS NOT PLANTED FULL grown in America. It was a slow growth beginning in Europe and developing further and more quickly in America. It did not envisage at first the man farthest down as a participant in democratic privilege or even as a possible participant. This was not simply because of the inability of the ignorant and degraded to express themselves and act intelligently and efficiently, but it was a failure to recognize that the mass of men had any rights which the better

---

1. At least this was the opinion of Abraham Lincoln—cf. Wilson's *Black Phalanx*, p. 108.

class were bound to respect. Thus democracy to the world first meant simply the transfer of privilege and opportunity from waning to waxing power, from the well-born to the rich, from the nobility to the merchants. Divine Right of birth yielded the Divine Right of wealth. Growing industry, business and commerce were putting economic and social power into the hands of what we call the middle class. Political opportunity to correspond with this power was the demand of the eighteenth century and this was what the eighteenth century called Democracy. On the other hand, both in Europe and in America, there were classes, and large classes, without power and without consideration whose place in democracy was inconceivable both to Europeans and Americans. Among these were the agricultural serfs and industrial laborers of Europe and the indentured servants and black slaves of America. The white serfs, as they were transplanted in America, began a slow, but in the end, effective agitation for recognition in American democracy. And through them has risen the modern American labor movement. But this movement almost from the first looked for its triumph along the ancient paths of aristocracy and sought to raise the white servant and laborer on the backs of the black servant and slave. If now the black man had been inert, unintelligent, submissive, democracy would have continued to mean in America what it means so widely still in Europe, the admission of the powerful to participation in government and privilege in so far and only in so far as their power becomes irresistible. It would not have meant a recognition of human beings as such and the giving of economic and social power to the powerless.

It is usually assumed in reading American history that whatever the Negro has done for America has been passive and unintelligent, that he accompanied the explorers as a beast of burden and accomplished whatever he did by sheer accident; that he labored because he was driven to labor and fought because he was made to fight. This is not true. On the contrary, it was the rise and growth among the slaves of a determination to be free and an active part of American democracy that forced American democracy continually to look into the depths; that held the faces of American thought to the inescapable fact that as long as there was a slave in America, America could not be a free republic; and more than that: as long as there were people in America, slave or nominally free, who could not participate in government and industry and society as free, intelligent human beings, our democracy had failed of its greatest mission.

This great vision of the black man was, of course, at first the vision of the few, as visions always are, but it was always there; it grew continuously and it developed quickly from wish to active determination. One cannot think then of democracy in America or in the modern world without reference to the American Negro. The democracy established in America in the eighteenth century was not, and was not designed to be, a democracy of the masses of men and it was thus singularly easy for people to fail to see the incongruity of democracy and slavery. It was the Negro himself who forced the consideration of this incongruity, who made emancipation inevitable and made the modern world at least consider if not wholly accept the idea of a democracy including men of all races and colors.

2. Influence on White Thought

NATURALLY, AT FIRST, IT WAS the passive presence of the Negro with his pitiable suffering and sporadic expression of unrest that bothered the American colonists. Massachusetts and Connecticut early in the seventeenth century tried to compromise with their consciences by declaring that there should be no slavery except of persons "willingly selling themselves" or "sold to us." And these were to have "All the liberties and Christian usages which the law of God established in Israel." Massachusetts even took a strong stand against proven "man stealing"; but it was left to a little band of Germans in Pennsylvania, in 1688, to make the first clear statement the moment they looked upon a black slave: "Now, though they are black, we cannot conceive there is more liberty to have them slaves than it is to have other white ones. There is a saying that we shall do to all men like as we will be done to ourselves, making no difference of what generation, descent or color they are. Here is liberty of conscience which is right and reasonable. Here ought also to be liberty of the body."[2]

In the eighteenth century, Sewall of Massachusetts attacked slavery. From that time down until 1863 man after man and prophet after prophet spoke against slavery and they spoke not so much as theorists but as people facing extremely uncomfortable facts. Oglethorpe would keep slavery out of Georgia because he saw how the strength of South Carolina went to defending themselves against possible

---

2. Thomas, *Attitude of Friends toward Slavery,* p. 267 and Appendix.

W.E.B. DU BOIS

slave insurrection rather than to defending the English colonies against the Spanish. The matter of baptizing the heathen whom slavery was supposed to convert brought tremendous heart searchings and argument and disputations and explanatory laws throughout the colonies. Contradictory benevolences were evident as when the Society for the Propagation of the Gospel sought to convert the Negroes and American legislatures sought to make the perpetual slavery of the converts sure.

The religious conscience, especially as it began to look upon America as a place of freedom and refuge, was torn by the presence of slavery. Late in the eighteenth and early in the nineteenth centuries pressure began to be felt from the more theoretical philanthropists of Europe and the position of American philanthropists was made correspondingly uncomfortable. Benjamin Franklin pointed out some of the evils of slavery; James Otis inveighing against England's economic tyranny acknowledged the rights of black men. Patrick Henry said that slavery was "repugnant to the first impression of right and wrong" and George Washington hoped slavery might be abolished. Thomas Jefferson made the celebrated statement: "Indeed I tremble for my country when I reflect that God is just; that His justice cannot sleep forever; that considering numbers, nature, and natural means only, a revolution of the wheel of fortune, an exchange of situation, is among possible events; that it may become probable by supernatural interference! The Almighty has no attribute which can take side with us in such a contest."[3]

Henry Laurens said to his son: "You know, my dear son, I abhor slavery. I was born in a country where slavery had been established by British kings and parliaments, as well as by the laws of that country ages before my existence. I found the Christian religion and slavery growing under the same authority and cultivation. I nevertheless disliked it. In former days there was no combating the prejudices of men supported by interest; the day I hope is approaching when, from principles of gratitude as well as justice, every man will strive to be foremost in showing his readiness to comply with the golden rule."[4]

The first draft of the Declaration of Independence harangued King George III of Britain for the presence of slavery in the United States:

---

3. Jefferson's Writings, Vol. 8, pp. 403–4.
4. George Livermore, *Opinions of the Founders of the Republic on Negroes as Slaves, as Citizens, and as Soldiers*, Boston, 1862, p. 61.

"He has waged cruel war against human nature itself, violating its most sacred rights of life and liberty in the persons of a distant people who never offended him; captivating and carrying them into slavery in another hemisphere, or to incur miserable death in their transportation thither. This piratical warfare, the opprobrium of Infidel powers, is the warfare of the Christian king of Great Britain. Determined to keep open market where men should be bought and sold, he has prostituted his negative for suppressing every legislative attempt to prohibit or to restrain this execrable commerce. And, that this assemblage of horrors might want no fact of distinguished die, he is now exciting those very people to rise in arms among us, and to purchase that liberty of which he has deprived them, by murdering the people on whom we also obtruded them; thus paying off former crimes committed against the liberties of one people with crimes which he urges them to commit against the lives of another."[5]

The final draft of the Declaration said: "We hold these truths to be self-evident:—that all men are created equal, that they are endowed by their Creator with certain inalienable rights; that among these are life, liberty, and the pursuit of happiness. That to secure these rights, governments are instituted among men, deriving their just powers from the consent of the governed."

It was afterward argued that Negroes were not included in this general statement and Judge Taney in his celebrated decision said in 1857:

"They had for more than a century before been regarded as beings of an inferior order, and altogether unfit to associate with the white race, either in social or political relations; and so far inferior that they had no rights which the white man was bound to respect; and that the Negro might justly and lawfully be reduced to slavery for his benefit. . ."[6]

This *obiter dictum* was disputed by equally learned justices. Justice McLean said in his opinion:

"Our independence was a great epoch in the history of freedom; and while I admit the Government was not made especially for the colored race, yet many of them were citizens of the New England States, and exercised the rights of suffrage when the Constitution was adopted; and

---

5. Jefferson's Works, Vol. 1, pp. 23–4.

6. Howard's Reports, Vol. 19.

it was not doubted by any intelligent person that its tendencies would greatly ameliorate their condition."[7]

Justice Curtis also said:

"It has been often asserted, that the Constitution was made exclusively by and for the white race. It has already been shown that in five of the thirteen original States, colored persons then possessed the elective franchise and were among those by whom the Constitution was ordained and established. If so, it is not true, in point of fact, that the Constitution was made exclusively by the white race. And that it was made exclusively for the white race is, in my opinion, not only an assumption not warranted by anything in the Constitution, but contradicted by its opening declaration, that it was ordained and established by the people of the United States, for themselves and their posterity. And, as free colored persons were then citizens of at least five States, they were among those for whom and whose posterity the Constitution was ordained and established."[8]

After the Revolution came the series of State acts abolishing slavery, beginning with Vermont in 1777; and then came the pause and retrogression followed by the slow but determined rise of the Cotton Kingdom. But even in that day the prophets protested. Hezekiah Niles said in 1819: "We are ashamed of the thing we practice; . . . there is no attribute of Heaven that takes part with us, and we know it. And in the contest that must come, and will come, there will be a heap of sorrows such as the world has rarely seen."[9] While the wild preacher, Lorenzo Dow, raised his cry from the wilderness even in Alabama and Mississippi, saying: "In the rest of the Southern States the influence of these Foreigners will be known and felt in its time, and the seeds from the HORY ALLIANCE and the DECAPIGANDI, who have a hand in those grades of Generals, from the Inquisitor to the Vicar General and down. . . The STRUGGLE will be DREADFUL! The CUP will be BITTER! and when the agony is over, those who survive may see better days! FAREWELL!"[10] Finally came William Lloyd Garrison and John Brown.

---

7. Howard's Reports, pp. 536–8.
8. Howard's Reports, pp. 572–3, 582.
9. Niles' Register, Vol. 16, May 22, 1819.
10. Benjamin Brawley, *A Social History of the American Negro,* New York, 1921, p. 90.

3. Insurrection

IT MAY BE SAID, AND it usually has been said, that all this showed the natural conscience and humanity of white Americans protesting and eventually triumphing over political and economic temptations. But to this must be added the inescapable fact that the attitude, thought and action of the Negro himself was in the largest measure back of this heart searching, discomfort and warning; and first of all was the physical force which the Negro again and again and practically without ceasing from the first days of the slave trade down to the war of emancipation, used to effect his own freedom.

We must remember that the slave trade itself was war; that from surreptitious kidnapping of the unsuspecting it was finally organized so as to set African tribes warring against tribes, giving the conquerors the actual aid of European or Arabian soldiers and the tremendous incentive of high prices for results of successful wars through the selling of captives. The captives themselves fought to the last ditch. It is estimated that every single slave finally landed upon a slave ship meant five corpses either left behind in Africa or lost through rebellion, suicide, sickness, and murder on the high seas. This which is so often looked upon as passive calamity was one of the most terrible and vindictive and unceasing struggles against misfortune that a group of human beings ever put forth. It cost Negro Africa perhaps sixty million souls to land ten million slaves in America.

The first influence of the Negro on American Democracy was naturally force to oppose force—revolt, murder, assassination coupled with running away. It was the primitive, ancient effort to avenge blood with blood, to bring good out of evil by opposing evil with evil. Whether right or wrong, effective or abortive, it is the human answer to oppression which the world has tried for thousands of years.

Two facts stand out in American history with regard to slave insurrections: on the one hand, there is no doubt of the continuous and abiding fear of them. The slave legislation of the Southern States is filled with ferocious efforts to guard against this. Masters were everywhere given peremptory and unquestioned power to kill a slave or even a white servant who should "resist his master." The Virginia law of 1680 said: "If any Negro or other slave shall absent himself from his master's service and lie, hide and lurk in obscure places, committing injuries to the inhabitants, and shall resist any person or persons that shall by lawful authority be employed to apprehend and take the said Negro, that then, in case of such resistance, it shall be lawful for such person or persons to kill the said Negro or slave so lying out and resisting."[11]

In 1691 and in 1748, there were Virginia acts to punish conspiracies and insurrections of slaves. In 1708 and in 1712 New York had laws against conspiracies and insurrections of Negroes. North Carolina passed such a law in 1741, and South Carolina in 1743 was legislating "against the insurrection and other wicked attempts of Negroes and other slaves." The Mississippi code of 1839 provides for slave insurrections "with arms in the intent to regain their liberty by force." Virginia in 1797 decreed death for any one exciting slaves to insurrection. In 1830 North Carolina made it a felony to incite insurrection among slaves. The penal code of Texas, passed in 1857, had a severe section against insurrection.[12]

Such legislation, common in every slave state, could not have been based on mere idle fear, and when we follow newspaper comment, debates and arguments and the history of insurrections and attempted insurrections among slaves, we easily see the reason. No sooner had the Negroes landed in America than resistance to slavery began.

As early as 1503 the Governor of Hispaniola stopped the transportation of Negroes "because they fled to the Indians and taught them bad manners and they could never be apprehended." In 1518 in the sugar mills of Haiti the Negroes "quit working and fled whenever they could in squads and started rebellions and committed murders." In 1522 there was a rebellion on the sugar plantations. Twenty Negroes from Diego Columbus' mill fled and killed several Spaniards. They joined with other rebellious Negroes on neighboring plantations. In 1523 many Negro slaves "fled to the Zapoteca and walked rebelliously through the country." In 1527 there was an uprising of Indians and Negroes in Florida. In 1532 the Wolofs and other rebellious Negroes caused insurrection among the Carib Indians. These Wolofs were declared to be "haughty, disobedient, rebellious and incorrigible." In 1548 there was a rebellion in Honduras and the Viceroy Mendoza in Mexico writes of an uprising among the slaves and Indians in 1537.[13] One of the most remarkable cases of resistance was the establishment and defense of

---

11. Hening's Statutes.
12. John C. Hurd, *The Law of Freedom and Bondage,* Boston, 1858–1862.
13. Wiener, *Africa and the Discovery of America,* Vol. 1, pp. 155–8.

Palmares in Brazil where 40 determined Negroes in 1560 established a city state which lived for nearly a half century growing to a population of 20,000 and only overthrown when 7,000 soldiers with artillery were sent against it. The Chiefs committed suicide rather than surrender.[14]

Early in the sixteenth century and from that time down until the nineteenth the black rebels whom the Spanish called "Cimarrones" and whom we know as "Maroons" were infesting the mountains and forests of the West Indies and South America. Gage says between 1520 and 1530: "What the Spaniards fear most until they get out of these mountains are two or three hundred Negroes, Cimarrones, who for the bad treatment they received have fled from masters in order to resort to these woods; there they live with their wives and children and increase in numbers every year, so that the entire force of Guatemala (City) and its environments is not capable to subdue them." Gage himself was captured by a mulatto corsair who was sweeping the seas in his own ship.[15]

The history of these Maroons reads like romance.[16] When England took Jamaica, in 1565, they found the mountains infested with Maroons whom they fought for ten years and finally, in 1663, acknowledged their freedom, gave them land and made their leader, Juan de Bolas, a colonel in the militia. He was killed, however, in the following year and from 1664 to 1778 some 3,000 black Maroons were in open rebellion against the British Empire. The English fought them with soldiers, Indians, and dogs and finally again, in 1738, made a formal treaty of peace with them, recognizing their freedom and granting them 25,000 acres of land. The war again broke out in 1795 and blood-hounds were again imported. The legislature wished to deport them but as they could not get their consent, peace was finally made on condition that the Maroons surrender their arms and settle down. No sooner, however, had they done this than the whites treacherously seized 600 of them and sent them to Nova Scotia. The Legislature voted a sword to the English general, who made the treaty; but he indignantly refused to accept it. Eventually these Maroons were removed to Sierra Leone where they saved that colony to the British by helping them put down an insurrection.

14. C. E. Chapman in *Journal of Negro History*, Vol. 3, p. 29.

15. J. Kunst, *Negroes in Guatemala, Journal of Negro History*, Vol. 1, pp. 392–8.

16. Cf. Bryan Edward's *West Indies*, 4th Edition, Vol. 1, pp. 337–98.

In the United States insurrection and attempts at insurrection among the slaves extended from Colonial times down to the Civil War. For the most part they were unsuccessful. In many cases the conspiracies were insignificant in themselves but exaggerated by fear of the owners. And yet a record of the attempts at revolt large and small is striking.

In Virginia there was a conspiracy in 1710 in Surrey County. In 1712 the City of New York was threatened with burning by slaves. In 1720 whites were attacked in the homes and on the streets in Charleston, S. C. In 1730 both in South Carolina and Virginia, slaves were armed to kill the white people and they planned to burn the City of Boston in 1723. In 1730 there was an insurrection in Williamsburg, Va., and five counties furnished armed men. In 1730 and 1731 homes were burned by slaves in Massachusetts and in Rhode Island and in 1731 and 1732 three ships crews were murdered by slaves. In 1729 the Governor of Louisiana reported that in an expedition sent against the Indians, fifteen Negroes had "performed prodigies of valor." But the very next year the Indians, led by a desperate Negro named Samba, were trying to exterminate the whites.[17] In 1741 an insurrection of slaves was planned in New York City, for which thirteen slaves were burned, eighteen hanged and eighty transported. In 1754 and 1755 slaves burned and poisoned certain masters in Charleston, S. C.[18]

4. Haiti and After

ON THE NIGHT OF AUGUST 23, 1791, the great Haitian rebellion took place. It had been preceded by a small rebellion of the mulattoes who were bitterly disappointed at the refusal of the planters to assent to what the free Negroes thought were the basic principles of the French Revolution. When 450,000 slaves joined them, they began a murderous civil war seldom paralleled in history. French, English and Spaniards participated. Toussaint, the first great black leader, was deceived, imprisoned and died perhaps by poisoning. Twenty-five thousand French soldiers were sent over by Napoleon Bonaparte to subdue the Negroes and begin the extension of his American empire through the West Indies and up the Mississippi valley. Despite all this, the Negroes

---

17. Gayarre, *History of Louisiana,* Vol. 1, pp. 435, 440.
18. Du Bois' *Slave Trade,* pp. 6, 10, 22, 206; J. Coppin, *Slave Insurrections,* 1860; Brawley, *Social History,* pp. 39, 86, 132.

were triumphant, established an independent state, made Napoleon give up his dream of American empire and sell Louisiana for a song:[19] "Thus, all of Indian Territory, all of Kansas and Nebraska and Iowa and Wyoming and Montana and the Dakotas, and most of Colorado and Minnesota, and all of Washington and Oregon states, came to us as the indirect work of a despised Negro. Praise if you will, the work of Robert Livingston or a Jefferson, but today let us not forget our debt to Toussaint L'Ouverture who was indirectly the means of America's expansion by the Louisiana Purchase of 1803."[20]

The Haitian revolution immediately had its effect upon both North and South America. We have read how Haitian volunteers helped in the American revolution. They returned to fight for their own freedom. Afterward when Bolivar, the founder of five free republics in South America, undertook his great rebellion in 1811 he at first failed. He took refuge in Jamaica and implored the help of England but was unsuccessful. Later in despair he visited Haiti. The black republic was itself at that time in a precarious position and had to act with great caution. Neverthless President Pétion furnished Bolivar, soldiers, arms and money. Bolivar embarked secretly and again sought to free South America. Again he failed and a second time returned to Haiti. Money and reinforcements were a second time furnished him and with the help of these achieved the liberation of Mexico and Central America.

Thus black Haiti not only freed itself but helped to kindle liberty all through America. Refugees from Haiti and San Domingo poured into the United States both colored and white and had great influence in Maryland and Louisiana.[21] Moreover the news of the black revolt filtered through to the slaves in the United States. Here the chains of slavery were stronger and the number of whites much larger. As I have said in another place: "A long, awful process of selection chose out the listless, ignorant, sly and humble and sent to heaven the proud, the vengeful and the daring. The old African warrior spirit died away of violence and a broken heart."[22]

Nevertheless a series of attempted rebellions took place which can be traced to the influence of Haiti. In 1800 came the Prosser conspiracy

---

19. Cf. T. G. Steward, *The Haitian Revolution.*
20. DeWitt Talmadge in the *Christian Herald,* Nov. 28, 1906; Du Bois' *Slave Trade,* Chapter 7.
21. Cf. Dunbar-Nelson in the *Journal of Negro History,* Vol. 1.
22. Du Bois, *John Brown,* p. 81.

in Virginia which planned a force of 11,000 Negroes to march in three columns in the city and seize the arsenal. A terrific storm thwarted these men and thirty-six were executed for the attempt. In 1791 Negroes of Louisiana sought to imitate Toussaint leading to the execution of twenty-three slaves. Other smaller attempts were made in South Carolina in 1816 and in Georgia in 1819. In 1822 came the celebrated attempt of Denmark Vesey, an educated freedman who through his trade as carpenter accumulated considerable wealth. He spoke French and English and was familiar with the Haitian revolution, the African Colonization scheme and the agitation attending the Missouri compromise. He openly discussed slavery and ridiculed the slaves for their cowardice and submission; he worked through the church and planned the total annihilation of the men, women and children of Charleston. Thousands of slaves were enrolled but one betrayed him and this led to the arrest of 137 blacks of whom 35 were hanged and 37 banished. A white South Carolinian writing after this plot said: "We regard our Negroes as the Jacobins of the country, against whom we should always be upon our guard and who although we fear no permanent effects from any insurrectionary movements on their part, should be watched with an eye of steady and unremitted observation."[23]

Less than ten years elapsed before another insurrection was planned and partially carried through. Its leader was Nat Turner, a slave born in Virginia in 1800. He was precocious and considered as "marked" by the Negroes. He had experimented in making paper, gun powder and pottery; never swore, never drank and never stole. For the most part he was a sort of religious devotee, fasting and praying and reading the Bible. Once he ran away but was commanded by spirit voices to return. By 1825 he was conscious of a great mission and on May 12, 1831, "a great voice said unto him that the serpent was loosed, that Christ had laid down the yoke." He believed that he, Nat Turner, was to lead the movement and that "the first should be last and the last first." An eclipse of the sun in February, 1831 was a further sign to him. He worked quickly. Gathering six friends together August 21, they made their plans and then started the insurrection by killing Nat's master and the family. About forty Negroes were gathered in all and they killed sixty-one white men, women and children. They were headed toward

---

23. A. H. Grimke, *Right on the Scaffold in Occasional Papers,* No. 7, American Negro Academy.

town when finally the whites began to arm in opposition. It was not, however, until two months later, October 30, that Turner himself was captured. He was tried November 5 and sentenced to be hanged. When asked if he believed in the righteousness of his mission he replied "Was not Christ crucified?" He made no confession.[24]

T. R. Grey—Turner's attorney—said "As to his ignorance, he certainly had not the advantages of education, but he can read and write and for natural intelligence and quickness of apprehension is surpassed by few men I have ever seen. Further the calm, deliberate composure with which he spoke of his late deeds and intentions, the expression of his fiend-like face when excited by enthusiasm; still bearing the stains of the blood of helpless innocence about him; clothed with rags and covered with chains, yet daring to raise his manacled hands to heaven; with a spirit soaring above the attributes of man, I looked on him and my blood curdled in my veins."[25]

Panic seized the whole of Virginia and the South. Military companies were mobilized, both whites and Negroes fled to the swamps, slaves were imprisoned and even as far down as Macon, Ga., the white women and children were guarded in a building against supposed insurrections. New slave codes were adopted, new disabilities put upon freedmen, the carrying of fire arms was especially forbidden. The Negro churches in the South were almost stopped from functioning and the Negro preachers from preaching. Traveling and meeting of slaves was stopped, learning to read and write was forbidden and incendiary pamphlets hunted down. Free Negroes were especially hounded, sold into slavery or driven out and a period of the worst oppression of the Negro in the land followed.

In 1839 and 1841 two cases of mutiny of slaves on the high seas caused much commotion in America. In 1839 a schooner, the Amistad, started from Havana for another West Indian port with 53 slaves. Led by a black man, Cinque, the slaves rose, killed the captain and some of the crew, allowed the rest of the crew to escape and put the two owners in irons. The Negroes then tried to escape to Africa, but after about two months they landed in Connecticut and a celebrated law case arose over the disposition of the black mutineers which went to the Supreme Court of the United States. John Quincy Adams defended them and won his case. Eventually money was raised and the Negroes returned to

24. Brawley, p. 140; T. W. Higginson, *Atlantic Monthly*, Vol. 8, p. 173.
25. I. W. Cromwell, in *Journal of Negro History*, Vol. 5, pp. 208ff.

Africa. While this case was in the court the brig Creole in 1841 sailed from Richmond to New Orleans with 130 slaves. Nineteen of the slaves mutinied and led by Madison Washington took command of the vessel and sailed to the British West Indies. Daniel Webster demanded the return of the slaves but the British authorities refused.

During these years, rebellion and agitation among Negroes, and agitation among white friends in Europe, was rapidly freeing the Negroes of the West Indies and beginning their incorporation into the body politic—a process not yet finished but which means possibly the eventual development of a free black and mulatto republic in the isles of the Caribbean.

It may be said that in most of these cases the attempts of the Negro to rebel were abortive, and this is true. Yet it must be remembered that in a few cases they had horrible success; in others nothing but accident or the actions of favorite slaves saved similar catastrophe, and more and more the white South had the feeling that it was sitting upon a volcano and that nothing but the sternest sort of repression would keep the Negro "in his place." The appeal of the Negro to force invited reaction and retaliation not only in the South, as we have noted, but also in the North. Here the common white workingman and particularly the new English, Scotch and Irish immigrants entirely misconceived the writhing of the black man. These white laborers, themselves so near slavery, did not recognize the struggle of the black slave as part of their own struggle; rather they felt the sting of economic rivalry and underbidding for home and job; they easily absorbed hatred and contempt for Negroes as their first American lesson and were flattered by the white capitalists, slave owners and sympathizers with slavery into lynching and clubbing their dark fellow victims back into the pit whence they sought to crawl. It was a scene for angels' tears.

In 1826 Negroes were attacked in Cincinnati and also in 1836 and 1841. At Portsmouth, Ohio, nearly one-half of the Negroes were driven out of the city in 1830 while mobs drove away free Negroes from Mercer County, Ohio. In Philadelphia, Negroes were attacked in 1820, 1830 and 1834, having their churches and property burned and ruined. In 1838 there was another anti-Negro riot and in 1842, when the blacks attempted to celebrate abolition in the West Indies. Pittsburg had a riot in 1839 and New York in 1843 and 1863.[26]

---

26. Cf. Du Bois' *Philadelphia Negro*, Chapter 4; Woodson's *Negro in our History*, pp. 140–1.

Thus we can see that the fear and heart searchings and mental upheaval of those who saw the anomaly of slavery in the United States was based not only upon theoretical democracy but on force and fear of force as used by the degraded blacks, and on the reaction of that appeal on southern legislatures and northern mobs.

5. The Appeal to Reason

THE APPEAL OF THE NEGRO to democracy, however, was not entirely or perhaps even principally an appeal of force. There was continually the appeal to reason and justice. Take the significant case of Paul Cuffee of Massachusetts, born in 1759, of a Negro father and Indian mother. When the selectmen of the town of Dartmouth refused to admit colored children to the public schools, or even to make separate provision for them, he refused to pay his school taxes. He was duly imprisoned, but when freed he built at his own expense a school house and opened it to all without race discrimination. His white neighbors were glad to avail themselves of this school as it was more convenient and just as good as the school in town. The result was that the colored children were soon admitted to all schools. Cuffee was a ship owner and trader, and afterward took a colony to Liberia at his own expense.[27] Again Prince Hall, the Negro founder of the African Lodge of Masons which the English set up in 1775, aroused by the revolution in Haiti and a race riot in Boston said in 1797:

"Patience, I say, for were we not possessed of a great measure of it you could not bear up under the daily insults you meet with in the streets of Boston; much more on public days of recreation, how are you shamefully abused, and that at such a degree that you may truly be said to carry your lives in your own hands. . .

"My brethren, let us not be cast down under these and many other abuses we at present labor under; for the darkest hour is before the break of day. My brethren, let us remember what a dark day it was with our African brethren six years ago, in the French West Indies. . . But blessed be to God, the scene is changed, they now confess that God hath no respect of persons, and therefore receive them as their friends and treat them as brothers. Thus doth Ethiopia begin to stretch forth her hand from a sink of slavery to freedom and equality."[28]

---

27. Brawley, pp. 123–4; *Journal of Negro History,* Vol. 2, pp. 209–28.
28. Brawley, p. 71.

A more subtle appeal was made by seven Massachusetts Negroes on taxation without representation. In a petition to the General Court of Massachusetts in 1780 they said: "We being chiefly of the African extract, and by reason of long bondage and hard slavery, we have been deprived of enjoying the profits of our labor or the advantage of inheriting estates from our parents, as our neighbors the white people do, having some of us not long enjoyed our own freedom; yet of late, contrary to the invariable custom and practice of the country, we have been, and now are, taxed both in our polls and that small pittance of estate which, through much hard labor and industry, we have got together to sustain ourselves and families withall. We apprehend it therefore, to be hard usage, and will doubtless (if continued) reduce us to a state of beggary, whereby we shall become a burden to others, if not timely prevented by the interposition of your justice and power.

"Your petitioners further show, that we apprehend ourselves to be aggrieved, in that, while we are not allowed the privilege of free men of the State, having no vote or influence in the election of those that tax us, yet many of our color (as is well known) have cheerfully entered the field of battle in the defence of the common cause, and that (as we conceive) against similar exertion of power (in regard to taxation) too well known to need a recital in this place."[29]

Perhaps though the most startling appeal and challenge came from David Walker, a free Negro, born of a free mother and slave father in North Carolina in 1785. He had some education, had traveled widely and conducted a second-hand clothing store in Boston in 1827. He spoke to various audiences of Negroes in 1828 and the following year published the celebrated "Appeal in four articles, together with a preamble to the Colored Citizens of the World but in particular and very expressly to those of the United States of America." It was a thin volume of 76 octavol pages, but it was frank and startlingly clear:

"Can our condition be any worse? Can it be more mean and abject? If there are any changes, will they not be for the better though they may appear for the worst at first? Can they get us any lower? Where can they get us? They cannot treat us worse; for they well know the day they do it they are gone. But against all accusations which may or can be preferred against me, I appeal to heaven for my motive in writing—who knows that my object is if possible to awaken in the breasts of my afflicted,

29. Williams' *Negro Race,* Vol. 2, p. 126.

degraded and slumbering brethren a spirit of enquiry and investigation respecting our miseries and wretchedness in this Republican land of Liberty! ! ! !

"My beloved brethren:—The Indians of North and South America—the Greeks—the Irish, subjected under the King of Great Britain—the Jews, that ancient people of the Lord—the inhabitants of the Islands of the Sea—in fine, all the inhabitants of the Earth, (except, however, the sons of Africa) are called men and of course are and ought to be free.—But we, (colored people) and our children are brutes and of course are and ought to be slaves to the American people and their children forever—to dig their mines and work their farms; and thus go on enriching them from one generation to another with our blood and our tears! ! ! !

"I saw a paragraph, a few years since, in a South Carolina paper, which, speaking of the barbarity of the Turks, it said: 'The Turks are the most barbarous people in the world—they treat the Greeks more like brutes than human beings.' And in the same paper was an advertisement which said: 'Eight well built Virginia and Maryland Negro fellows and four wenches will positively be sold this day to the highest bidder!'

"Beloved brethren—here let me tell you, and believe it, that the Lord our God as true as He sits on His throne in heaven and as true as our Saviour died to redeem the world, will give you a Hannibal, and when the Lord shall have raised him up and given him to you for your possession, Oh! my suffering brethren, remember the divisions and consequent sufferings of Carthage and of Haiti. Read the history particularly of Haiti and see how they were butchered by the whites and do you take warning. The person whom God shall give you, give him your support and let him go his length and behold in him the salvation of your God. God will indeed deliver you through him from your deplorable and wretched condition under the Christians of America. I charge you this day before my God to lay no obstacle in his way, but let him go. . . What the American preachers can think of us, I aver this day before my God I have never been able to define. They have newspapers and monthly periodicals which they receive in continual succession but on the pages of which you will scarcely ever find a paragraph respecting slavery which is ten thousand times more injurious to this country than all the other evils put together; and which will be the final overthrow of its government unless something is very speedily done; for their cup is nearly full.—Perhaps they will laugh at or make light of this; but I tell you, Americans! that unless you speedily alter your course, you and your Country are gone!

"Do you understand your own language? Hear your language proclaimed to the world, July 4, 1776—'We hold these truths to be self evident—that ALL men are created EQUAL!! That they are endowed by their Creator with certain unalienable rights; that among these are life, liberty and the pursuit of happiness!!! Compare your own language above, extracted from your Declaration of Independence, with your cruelties and murders inflicted by your cruel and unmerciful fathers and yourselves on our fathers and on us—men who have never given your fathers or you the least provocation!!!

"Now Americans! I ask you candidly, was your suffering under Great Britain one hundredth part as cruel and tryrannical as you have rendered ours under you? Some of you, no doubt, believe that we will never throw off your murderous government and provide new guards for our future 'security'. If Satan has made you believe it, will he not deceive you?"

The book had a remarkable career. It appeared in September, was in a third edition by the following March and aroused the South to fury. Special laws were passed and demands made that Walker be punished. He died in 1830, possibly by foul play.

6. The Fugitive Slave

BESIDE FORCE AND THE APPEAL to reason there was a third method which practically was more effective and decisive for eventual abolition, and that was the escape from slavery through running away. On the islands this meant escape to the mountains and existence as brigands. In South America it meant escape to the almost impenetrable forest.

As I have said elsewhere:[30]

"One thing saved the South from the blood sacrifice of Haiti—not, to be sure, from so successful a revolt, for the disproportion of races was less, but from a desperate and bloody effort—and that was the escape of the fugitive.

"Along the Great Black Way stretched swamps and rivers and the forests and crests of the Alleghanies. A widening, hurrying stream of fugitives swept to the havens of refuge, taking the restless, the criminal

---

30. Du Bois' *John Brown,* pp. 82ff.

and the unconquered—the natural leaders of the more timid mass. These men saved slavery and killed it. They saved it by leaving it to a false seductive dream of peace and the eternal subjugation of the laboring class. They destroyed it by presenting themselves before the eyes of the North and the world as living specimens of the real meaning of slavery."

"Three paths were opened to the slaves: to submit, to fight or to run away. Most of them submitted, as do most people everywhere, to force and fate. To fight singly meant death and to fight together meant plot and insurrection—a difficult thing, but one often tried. Easiest of all was to run away, for the land was wide and bare and the slaves were many. At first they ran to the swamps and mountains and starved and died. Then they ran to the Indians and in Florida founded a nation, to overthrow which cost the United States $20,000,000 and more in slave raids known as the Seminole 'wars.' Then gradually, after the War of 1812 had used so many black sailors to fight for free trade that the Negroes learned of the North and Canada as cities of refuge, they fled northward."

From the sixteenth century Florida Indians had Negro blood, but from early part of the nineteenth century the Seminoles gained a large new infiltration of Negro blood from the numbers of slaves who fled to them and with whom they intermarried. The first Seminole war, therefore, in 1818 was not simply a defense of the frontiers against the Indians and a successful raid to drive Spain from Florida, it was also a slave raid by Georgia owners determined to have back their property. By 1815 Negroes from Georgia among the Creeks and Seminoles numbered not less than 11,000 and were settled along the Appalachicola river, many of them with good farms and with a so-called Negro "fort" for protection. The war was disastrous to Negroes and Indians but not fatal and in 1822 some 800 Negroes were counted among the Indians who inhabited the new territory seized from Spain. Pressure to secure alleged fugitives and Negroes from the Indians was kept up for the next three years and the second Seminole war broke out because the whites treacherously seized the mulatto wife of the Indian chief Osceola. The war broke out in 1837 and its real nature, as a New Orleans paper said in 1839, was to subdue the Seminoles and decrease the danger of uprisings "among the serviles." Finally after a total cost of twenty million dollars the Indians were subdued and moved to the West and a part of the Negroes driven back into slavery, but not all.[31]

---

31. Cf. Joshua R. Giddings, *Exiles of Florida*, Columbus, Ohio, 1858.

Through the organization which came to be known as the Underground Railroad, thousands of slaves escaped through Kentucky and into the Middle West and thence into Canada and also by way of the Appalachian Mountains into Pennsylvania and the East. Not only were they helped by white abolitionists but they were guided by black men and women like Joshua Henson and Harriet Tubman.

Beside this there came the effort for emigration to Africa which was very early suggested. Two colored men sailed from New York for Africa in 1774 but the Revolutionary War stopped the effort thus begun. The Virginia legislature in secret session after Gabriel's insurrection in 1800, tried to suggest the buying of some land for the colonization of free Negroes, following the proposal of Thomas Jefferson made in 1781. Paul Cuffee, mentioned above, started the actual migration in 1815 carrying nine colored families, thirty-eight persons in all, to Sierra Leone at an expense of $4,000 which he paid himself. Finally came the American Colonization Society in 1817 but it was immediately turned from a real effort to abolish slavery gradually into an effort to get rid of free Negroes and obstreperous slaves. Even the South saw it and Robert Y. Hayne said in Congress: "While this process is going on, the colored classes are gradually diffusing themselves throughout the country and are making steady advances in intelligence and refinement and if half the zeal were displayed in bettering their condition that is now wasted in the vain and fruitless effort of sending them abroad, their intellectual and moral improvement would be steady and rapid."

7. Bargaining

THE NEGRO EARLY LEARNED A lesson which he may yet teach the modern world and which may prove his crowning gift to America and the world: Force begets force and you cannot in the end run away successfully from the world's problems. The Negro early developed the shrewd foresight of recognizing the fact that as a minority of black folk in a growing white country, he could not win his battle by force. Moreover, for the mass of Negroes it was impracticable to run away and find refuge in some other land.

Even the appeal to reason had its limitations in an unreasoning land. It could not unfortunately base itself on justice and right in the midst of the selfish, breathless battle to earn a living. There was however a chance to prove that justice and self interest sometimes go hand in hand. Force and flight might sometimes help but there was still the important method of co-operating with the best forces of the nation in order to help them to win and in order to prove that the Negro was a valuable asset, not simply as a laborer but as a worker for social uplift, as an American. Sometimes this co-operation was in simple and humble ways and nevertheless striking. There was, for instance, the yellow fever epidemic in Philadelphia in 1793. The blacks were not suffering from it or at least not supposed to suffer from it as much as the whites. The papers appealed to them to come forward and help with the sick. Led by Jones, Gray and Allen, Negroes volunteered their services and worked with the sick and in burying the dead, even spending some of their own funds in the gruesome duty. The same thing happened much later in New Orleans, Memphis and Cuba.

In larger ways it must be remembered that the Abolition crusade itself could not have been successful without the co-operation of Negroes. Black folk like Remond, Frederick Douglass, and Sojourner Truth, were not simply advocates for freedom but were themselves living refutations of the whole doctrine of slavery. Their appeal was tremendous in its efficiency and besides, the free Negroes helped by work and money to spread the Abolition campaign.[32]

In addition to this there was much deliberate bargaining,—careful calculation on the part of the Negro that if the whites would aid them, they in turn would aid the whites at critical times and that otherwise they would not. Much of this went on at the time of the Revolution and was clearly recognized by the whites.

Alexander Hamilton (himself probably of Negro descent) said in 1779: "The contempt we have been taught to entertain for the blacks makes us fancy many things that are founded neither in reason nor experience; and an unwillingness to part with property of so valuable a kind will furnish a thousand arguments to show the impracticability or pernicious tendency of a scheme which requires such a sacrifice. But it should be considered that if we do not make use of them in this way, the enemy probably will; and that the best way to counteract the temptations they will hold out will be to offer them ourselves. An essential part of the plan is to give them their freedom with their muskets. This will secure their fidelity, animate their courage, and, I

---

32. Among the first subscribers to Garrison's *Liberator* were free Negroes and one report is that the very first paid subscriber was a colored Philadelphia caterer.

believe, will have a good influence upon those who remain by opening a door to their emancipation. This circumstance, I confess, has no small weight in inducing me to wish the success of the project; for the dictates of humanity and true policy equally interest me in favor of this unfortunate class of men."[33]

Dr. Hopkins wrote in 1776: "God is so ordering it in His providence that it seems absolutely necessary something should speedily be done with respect to the slaves among us in order to our safety and to prevent their turning against us in our present struggle in order to get their liberty. Our oppressors have planned to gain the blacks and induce them to take up arms against us by promising them liberty on this condition; and this plan they are prosecuting to the utmost of their power. . . The only way pointed out to prevent this threatening evil is to set the blacks at liberty ourselves by some public acts and laws; and then give them proper encouragement to labor or take arms in the defense of the American cause, as they shall choose. This would at once be doing them some degree of justice and defeating our enemies in the scheme they are prosecuting."[34]

When Dunmore appealed to the slaves of Virginia at the beginning of the Revolution, the slave owners issued an almost plaintive counter appeal:

"Can it, then, be supposed that the Negroes will be better used by the English who have always encouraged and upheld this slavery than by their present masters who pity their condition; who wish, in general, to make it easy and comfortable as possible; and who would, were it in their power, or were they permitted, not only prevent any more Negroes from losing their freedom but restore it to such as have already unhappily lost it?"[35]

In the South, where Negroes for the most part were not received as soldiers, the losses of the slaveholders by defection among the slaves was tremendous. John Adams says that the Georgia delegates gave him "a melancholy account of the State of Georgia and South Carolina. They said if one thousand regular troops should land in Georgia and their commander be provided with arms and clothes enough and proclaim freedom to all the Negroes who would join his camp, twenty thousand

---

33. Livermore, p. 170.
34. Livermore, pp. 125–6.
35. Force's Archives, 4th series, Vol. 3, p. 1387.

Negroes would join it from the two provinces in a fortnight. The Negroes have a wonderful art of communicating intelligence among themselves; it will run several hundreds of miles in a week or fortnight. They said their only security was this,—that all the King's friends and tools of Government have large plantations and property in Negroes, so that the slaves of the Tories would be lost as well as those of the Whigs."[36]

Great Britain, after Cornwallis surrendered, even dreamed of reconquering America with Negroes. A Tory wrote to Lord Dunmore in 1782:

"If, my Lord, this scheme is adopted, arranged and ready for being put in execution, the moment the troops penetrate into the country after the arrival of the promised re-enforcements, America is to be conquered with its own force (I mean the Provincial troops and the black troops to be raised), and the British and Hessian army could be spared to attack the French where they are most vulnerable. . ."

"'What! Arm the slaves? We shudder at the very idea, so repugnant to humanity, so barbarous and shocking to human nature,' etc. One very simple answer is, in my mind, to be given: Whether it is better to make this vast continent become an acquisition of power, strength and consequence to Great Britain again, or tamely give it up to France who will reap the fruits of American independence to the utter ruin of Britain? . . . experience will, I doubt not, justify the assertion that by embodying the most hardy, intrepid and determined blacks, they would not only keep the rest in good order but by being disciplined and under command be prevented from raising cabals, tumults, and even rebellion, what I think might be expected soon after a peace; but so far from making even our lukewarm friends and secret foes greater enemies by this measure, I will, by taking their slaves, engage to make them better friends."[37]

On the other hand, the Colonial General Greene wrote to the Governor of South Carolina the same year:

"The natural strength of the country in point of numbers appears to me to consist much more in the blacks than in the whites. Could they be incorporated and employed for its defence, it would afford you double security. That they would make good soldiers, I have not the least doubt; and I am persuaded the State has it not in its power to give

36. Works of John Adams, Vol. 2, p. 428.
37. Livermore, pp. 183, 184.

sufficient re-enforcements without incorporating them either to secure the country if the enemy mean to act vigorously upon an offensive plan or furnish a force sufficient to dispossess them of Charleston should it be defensive."

This spirit of bargaining, more or less carefully carried out, can be seen in every time of stress and war. During the Civil War certain groups of Negroes sought repeatedly to make terms with the Confederacy. Judah Benjamin said at a public meeting in Richmond in 1865:

"We have 680,000 blacks capable of bearing arms and who ought now to be in the field. Let us now say to every Negro who wishes to go into the ranks on condition of being free, go and fight—you are free. My own Negroes have been to me and said, 'Master, set us free and we'll fight for you.' You must make up your minds to try this or see your army withdrawn from before your town. I know not where white men can be found."[38]

Robert E. Lee said: "We should not expect slaves to fight for prospective freedom when they can secure it at once by going to the enemy in whose service they will incur no greater risk than in ours. The reasons that induce me to recommend the employment of Negro troops at all render the effect of the measures I have suggested upon slavery immaterial and in my opinion the best means of securing the efficiency and fidelity of the auxiliary force would be to accompany the measure with a well-digested plan of gradual and general emancipation. As that will be the result of the continuance of the war and will certainly occur if the enemy succeed, it seems to me most advisable to adopt it at once and thereby obtain all the benefits that will accrue to our cause."

"The employment of Negro troops under regulations similar to those indicated would, in my opinion, greatly increase our military strength and enable us to relieve our white population to some extent. I think we could dispense with the reserve forces except in cases of emergency. It would disappoint the hopes which our enemies have upon our exhaustion, deprive them in a great measure of the aid they now derive from black troops and thus throw the burden of the war upon their own people. In addition to the great political advantages that would result to our cause from the adoption of a system of emancipation, it would exercise a salutary influence upon our Negro population by rendering

---

38. Wilson, pp. 491–92.

more secure the fidelity of those who become soldiers and diminishing inducements to the rest to abscond."[39]

At the time of the World War there was a distinct attitude on the part of the Negro population that unless they were recognized in the draft and had Negro officers and were not forced to become simply laborers, they would not fight and while expression of this determination was not always made openly it was recognized even by an administration dominated by Southerners. Especially were there widespread rumors of German intrigue among Negroes, which had some basis of fact.

Within the Negro group every effort for organization and uplift was naturally an effort toward the development of American democracy. The motive force of democracy has nearly always been the push from below rather than the aristocratic pull from above; the effort of the privileged classes to outstrip the surging forward of the bourgeoisie has made groups and nations rise; the determination of the "poor whites" in the South not to be outdone by the "nigger" has been caused by the black man's frantic efforts to rise rather than by any innate ambition on the part of the lower class of whites. It was a push from below and it made the necessity of recognizing the white laborer even more apparent. The great democratic movement which took place during the reign of Andrew Jackson from 1829–1837 was caused in no small degree by the persistent striving of the Negroes. They began their meeting together in conventions in 1830, they organized migration to Canada.[40] In the trouble with Canada in 1837 and 1838 Negro refugees from America helped to defend the frontiers. Bishop Loguen says: "The colored population of Canady at that time was small compared to what it now is; nevertheless, it was sufficiently large to attract the attention of the government. They were almost to a man fugitives from the States. They could not, therefore, be passive when the success of the invaders would break the only arm interposed for their security, and destroy the only asylum for African freedom in North America. The promptness with which several companies of blacks were organized and equipped, and the desperate valor they displayed in this brief conflict, are an earnest of what may be expected from the welling thousands of colored fugitives collecting there, in the event of a war between the two countries."[41]

---

39. J. T. Wilson, *The History of the Black Phalanx*, Hartford, 1897, p. 490.
40. Cf. Cromwell, *Negro in American History*, Chapter 2.
41. J. W. Loguen, *As a Slave and as a Freeman*, p. 344.

In America during this time they sought to establish a manual training college, they established their first weekly newspaper and they made a desperate fight for admission to the schools. They helped thus immeasurably the movement for universal popular education, joined the antislavery societies and organized churches and beneficial societies; bought land and continued to appeal. Wealthy free Negroes began to appear even in the South, as in the case of Jehu Jones, proprietor of a popular hotel in Charleston, and later Thomé Lafon of New Orleans who accumulated nearly a half million dollars and eventually left it to Negro charities which still exist. In the North there were tailors and lumber merchants and the guild of the caterers; taxable property slowly but surely increased.

All this in a peculiar way forced a more all-embracing democracy upon America, and it blossomed to fuller efficiency after the Civil War.

V

The Reconstruction of Freedom

How the black fugitive, soldier and freedman after the Civil War helped to restore the Union, establish public schools, enfranchise the poor white and initiate industrial democracy in America.

There have been four great steps toward democracy taken in America: The refusal to be taxed by the English Parliament; the escape from European imperialism; the discarding of New England aristocracy; and the enfranchisement of the Negro slave.

What did the Emancipation of the slave really mean? It meant such property rights as would give him a share in the income of southern industry large enough to support him as a modern free laborer; and such a legal status as would enable him by education and experience to bear his responsibility as a worker and citizen. This was an enormous task and meant the transformation of a slave holding oligarchy into a modern industrial democracy.

Who could do this? Some thought it done by the Emancipation Proclamation and the 13th amendment and Garrison with naive faith in bare law abruptly stopped the issue of the *Liberator* when the slave was declared "free." The Negro was not freed by edict or sentiment but by the Abolitionists backed by the persistent action of the slave himself as fugitive, soldier and voter.

Slavery was the cause of the war. There might have been other questions large enough and important enough to have led to a disruption of the Union but none have successfully done so except slavery. But the North fought for union and not against slavery and for a long time it refused to recognize that the Civil War was essentially a war against Negro slavery. Abraham Lincoln said to Horace Greeley as late as August, 1862, "If there be those who would not save the Union unless they could at the same time destroy slavery, I do not agree with them. My paramount object is to save the Union and not either to save or destroy slavery."

Despite this attitude it was evident very soon that the Nation was fighting against the symptom of disease and not against the cause. If we look at the action of the North taken by itself, we find these singular contradictions: They fought for the Union; they suddenly emancipated the slave; they enfranchised the Freedmen; they abandoned the Freedmen. If now this had been the deliberate action of the North it would have been a crazy program; but it was not. The action of the American Negro himself forced the nation into many of these various contradictions; and the motives of the Negro were primarily economic. He was trying to achieve economic emancipation. And it is this fact that makes Reconstruction one of the greatest attempts to spread democracy which the modern world has seen.

There were in the South in 1860, 3,838,765 Negro slaves and 258,346 free Negroes. The question of land and fugitive slaves had precipitated the war: that is, if slavery was to survive it had to have more slave territory, and this the North refused. Moreover if slavery was to survive the drain of fugitive slaves must stop or the slave trade be reopened. The North refused to consider the reopening of the slave trade and only half-heartedly enforced the fugitive slave laws.

No sooner then did the war open in April, 1861, than two contradictory things happened: Fugitive slaves began to come into the lines of the Union armies at the very time that Union Generals were assuring the South that slavery would not be interfered with. In Virginia, Colonel Tyler said "The relation of master and servant as recognized in your state shall be respected." At Port Royal, General T. W. Sherman declared that he would not interfere with "Your social and local institution." Dix in Virginia refused to admit fugitive slaves within his lines and Halleck in Missouri excluded them. Later, both Buell at Nashville and Hooker on the upper Potomac allowed their camps to be searched by masters for fugitive slaves.[1]

Against this attitude, however, there appeared, even in the first year of the War, some unanswerable considerations. For instance three slaves escaped into General Butler's lines at Fortress Monroe just as they were about to be sent to North Carolina to work on Confederate fortifications. Butler immediately said "These men are contraband of war, set them at work." Butler's action was sustained.[2] But when Fremont, in August freed the slaves of Missouri under martial law, declaring

---

1. George W. Williams, *History of the Negro Race in America*, New York, 1882, Vol. 1, Chapter 15.
2. Williams, Vol. 1, pp. 250–1.

it an act of war, Lincoln hastened to repudiate his action;[3] and the same thing happened the next year when Hunter at Hilton Head, S. C. declared "Slavery and martial law in a free country. . . incompatible."[4] Nevertheless here loomed difficulty and the continued coming of the fugitive slaves increased the difficulty and forced action.

The year 1862 saw the fugitive slave recognized as a worker and helper within the Union lines and eventually as a soldier bearing arms. Thousands of black men during that year, of all ages and both sexes, clad in rags and with their bundles on their backs, gathered wherever the Union Army gained foothold—at Norfolk, Hampton, at Alexandria and Nashville and along the border towards the West. There was sickness and hunger and some crime but everywhere there was desire for employment. It was in vain that Burnside was insisting that slavery was not to be touched and that McClellan repeated this on his Peninsular Campaign.

A change of official attitude began to appear as indeed it had to. When for instance General Saxton, with headquarters at Beauford, S. C., took military control of that district, he began to establish market houses for the sale of produce from the plantations and to put the Negroes to work as wage laborers. When, in the West, Grant's army occupied Grand Junction, Mississippi and a swarm of fugitives appeared, naked and hungry, some were employed as teamsters, servants and cooks and finally Grant appointed a "Chief of Negro affairs" for the entire district under his jurisdiction. Crops were harvested, wages paid, wood cutters swarmed in forests to furnish fuel for the Federal gun-boats, cabins were erected and a regular "Freedmen's Bureau" came gradually into operation. The Negroes thus employed as regular helpers and laborers in the army, swelled to more than 200,000 before the end of the war; and if we count transient workers and spies who helped with information, the number probably reached a half million.

If now the Negro could work for the Union Army why could he not also fight? We have seen in the last chapter how the nation hesitated and then yielded in 1862. The critical Battle of Antietam took place September 17th and the confederate avalanche was checked. Five days later, Abraham Lincoln proclaimed that he was going to recommend an appropriation by Congress for encouraging the gradual abolition

---

3. Williams, Vol. 2, pp. 255–7.
4. Williams, Vol. 1, pp. 257–9.

of slavery through payment for the slaves; and that on the following January 1st, in all the territory which was still at war with the United States, he proposed to declare the slaves free as a military measure.[5] Thus the year 1862 saw the Negro as an active worker in the army and as a soldier.

This fact together with the Emancipation Proclamation of January 1st, made the year 1863 a significant year. Not only were most of the slaves legally freed by military edict but by the very fact of their emancipation the stream of fugitives became a vast flood. The Army had to organize departments and appoint officials for the succor and guidance of these fugitives in their work; relief on a large scale began to appear from the North and the demand of the Negro for education began to be felt in the starting of schools here and there.

"The fugitives poured into the lines and gradually were used as laborers and helpers. Immediately teaching began and gradually schools sprang up. When at last the Emancipation Proclamation was issued and Negro soldiers called for, it was necessary to provide more systematically for Negroes. Various systems and experiments grew up here and there. The Freedmen were massed in large numbers at Fortress Monroe, Va., Washington, D. C., Beaufort and Port Royal, S. C., New Orleans, La., Vicksburg and Corinth, Miss., Columbus, Ky., Cairo, Ill., and elsewhere. In such places schools immediately sprang up under the army officers and chaplains. The most elaborate system, perhaps, was that under General Banks in Louisiana. It was established in 1863 and soon had a regular Board of Education, which laid and collected taxes and supported eventually nearly a hundred schools with ten thousand pupils, under 162 teachers. At Port Royal, S. C., were gathered Edward L. Pierce's 'Ten Thousand Clients' . . . In the west, General Grant appointed Colonel John Eaton, afterwards United States Commissioner of Education to be Superintendent of Freedmen in 1862. He sought to consolidate and regulate the schools already established and succeeded in organizing a large system."[6]

The Treasury Department of the Government, solicitous for the cotton crop, took charge of certain plantations in order to encourage the workers and preserve the crop. Thus during the Spring of 1863, there were groups of Freedmen and refugeesin long broken lines

5. Preliminary Emancipation Proclamation, Sept. 22, 1862.
6. Atlanta University Publications, Atlanta, Ga., 1906, No. 8, p. 23.

between the two armies reaching from Maryland to the Kansas border and down the coast from Norfolk to New Orleans.

In 1864 a significant action took place: the petty and insulting discrimination in the pay of white and colored soldiers was stopped. The Negro began to be a free man and the center of the problem of Emancipation became land and organized industry. Eaton, the Superintendent of Freedmen reports, July 15, for his particular district:

"These Freedmen are now disposed of as follows: In military service as soldiers' laundresses, cooks, officers' servants and laborers in the various staff departments, 41,150; in cities, on plantations and in freedmen's villages and cared for, 72,500. Of these 62,300 are entirely self-supporting—the same as any individual class anywhere else—as planters, mechanics, barbers, hackmen, draymen, etc., conducting on their own responsibility or working as hired laborers. The remaining 10,200 receive subsistence from the government. Three thousand of them are members of families whose heads are carrying on plantations and have under cultivation 4,000 acres of cotton. They are to pay the government for their subsistence from the first income of the crop. The other 7,200 include the paupers, that is to say, all Negroes over and under the self-supporting age, the crippled and sick in hospitals, of the 113,650, and those engaged in their care. Instead of being unproductive this class has now under cultivation 500 acres of corn, 970 acres of vegetables and 1,500 acres of cotton besides working at wood-chopping and other industries. There are reported in the aggregate over 100,000 acres of cotton under cultivation. Of these about 7,000 acres are leased and cultivated by blacks. Some Negroes are managing as high as 300 or 400 acres. . ."[7]

The experiment at Davis Bend, Mississippi, was of especial interest: "Late in the season—in November and December, 1864,—the Freedmen's Department was restored to full control over the camps and plantations on President's Island and Palmyra or Davis Bend. Both these points had been originally occupied at the suggestion of General Grant and were among the most successful of our enterprises for the Negroes. With the expansion of the lessee system, private interests were allowed to displace the interest of the Negroes whom we had established there under the protection of the government, but orders issued by General N. J. T. Dana, upon whose sympathetic and intelligent co-operation my officers could always rely, restored to us the

7. John Eaton, *Grant, Lincoln and the Freedmen,* New York, 1907, p. 134.

W.E.B. DU BOIS

full control of these lands. The efforts of the freedmen on Davis Bend were particularly encouraging, and this property under Colonel Thomas' able direction, became in reality the "Negro Paradise" that General Grant had urged us to make of it."[8]

The United States Treasury went further in overseeing Freedmen and abandoned lands and appointed special agents over "Freedmen's home colonies." Down the Mississippi Valley, General Thomas issued a lengthy series of instructions covering industry. He appointed three Commissioners to lease plantations and care for the employees; fixed the rate of wages and taxed cotton. At Newbern, N. C., there were several thousand refugees to whom land was assigned and about 800 houses rented. After Sherman's triumphant March to the Sea, Secretary Stanton himself went to Savannah to investigate the condition of the Negroes.

It was significant that even this early Abraham Lincoln himself was suggesting limited Negro suffrage. Already he was thinking of the reconstruction of the states; Louisiana had been in Union hands for two years and Lincoln wrote to Governor Hahn, March 13th, 1864: "Now you are about to have a convention, which, . . . will probably define the elective franchise. I barely suggest, for your private consideration, whether some of the colored people may not be let in, as, for instance, the very intelligent, and especially those who have fought gallantly in our ranks. They would probably help, in some trying time to come, to keep the jewel of liberty within the family of freedom. But this is only a suggestion, not to the public, but to you alone."[9]

Here again the development had been logical. The Negroes were voting in many Northern states. At least one-half million of them were taking part in the war, nearly 200,000 as armed soldiers. They were beginning to be reorganized in industry by the army officials as free laborers. Naturally the question must come sooner or later: Could they be expected to maintain their freedom, either political or economic, unless they had a vote? And Lincoln with rare foresight saw this several months before the end of the war.

The year 1865 brought fully to the front the question of Negro suffrage and Negro free labor. They were recognized January 16th, when Sherman settled large numbers of Negroes on the Sea Islands. His order said:

---

8. Eaton, 165.
9. Walter L. Fleming, *Documentary History of Reconstruction,* Cleveland, Ohio, 1907, Vol. 1, p. 112.

"The Islands from Charleston, south, the abandoned rice fields along the rivers for thirty miles from the sea, and the country bordering the St. John's river, Florida, are reserved and set apart for the settlement of the Negroes now made free by the acts of war and the proclamation of the President of the United States.

"At Beaufort, Hilton Head, Savannah, Fernandina, St. Augustine, and Jacksonville, the blacks may remain in their chosen or accustomed vocations but on the islands, and in the settlements hereafter to be established, no white person whatever, unless military officers and soldiers detailed for duty, will be permitted to reside; and the sole and exclusive management of affairs will be left to the freed people themselves, subject only to the United States military authority and the acts of Congress. By the laws of war and orders of the President of the United States the Negro is free, and must be dealt with as such. He cannot be subjected to conscription or forced military service, save by the written orders of the highest military authority of the department, under such regulations as the President or Congress may prescribe. Domestic servants, blacksmiths, carpenters, and other mechanics, will be free to select their own work and residence, but the young and able-bodied Negroes must be encouraged to enlist as soldiers in the service of the United States, to contribute their share towards maintaining their own freedom, and securing their rights as citizens of the United States.

"Whenever three respectable Negroes, heads of families shall desire to settle on lands, and shall have selected for that purpose an island or a locality clearly defined, within the limits above designated, the Inspector of Settlements and Plantations will himself, or by such subordinate officer as he may appoint, give them a license to settle such island or district, and afford them such assistance as he can to enable them to establish a peaceful agricultural settlement. The three parties named will subdivide the land, under the supervision of the Inspector, among themselves and such others as may choose to settle near them, so that each family shall have a plot of not more than forty (40) acres of tillable ground, and when it borders on some water channel, with not more than 800 feet water front, in the possession of which land the military authorities will afford them protection until such time as they can protect themselves, or until Congress shall regulate their title."[10]

---

10. Fleming, Vol. 1, pp. 350–1.

W.E.B. DU BOIS

On March 3, 1865 the Nation came to the parting of the ways. Two measures passed Congress on this momentous date. First, a Freedmen's Bank was incorporated at Washington "to receive on deposit therefore, by or on behalf of persons heretofore held in slavery in the United States or their descendants, and investing the same in the stocks, bonds, Treasury notes, or other securities of the United States."[11] The first year it had $300,000 of deposits and the deposits increased regularly until in 1871 there were nearly $20,000,000. Also on March 3rd, the Freedmen's Bureau Act was passed. The war was over. Sometime the South must have restored home rule. When that came what would happen to the freedmen?

These paths were before the nation:

1. They might abandon the freedman to the mercy of his former masters.
2. They might for a generation or more make the freedmen the wards of the nation—protecting them, encouraging them, educating their children, giving them land and a minimum of capital and thus inducting them into real economic and political freedom.
3. They might force a grant of Negro suffrage, support the Negro voters for a brief period and then with hands off let them sink or swim.

The second path was the path of wisdom and statesmanship. But the country would not listen to such a comprehensive plan. If the form of this Bureau had been worked out by Charles Sumner today instead of sixty years ago, it would have been regarded as a proposal far less revolutionary than the modern labor legislation of America and Europe. A half-century ago, however, and in a country which gave the *laisser-faire* economics their extremest trial the Freedmen's Bureau struck the whole nation as unthinkable save as a very temporary expedient and to relieve the more pointed forms of distress following war. Yet the proposals of the Bureau as actually established by the laws of 1865 and 1866 were both simple and sensible:

1. To oversee the making and enforcement of wage contracts.
2. To appear in the courts as the freedmen's best friend.

---

11. Fleming, Vol. 2, p. 382.

3. To furnish the freedmen with a minimum of land and of capital.
4. To establish schools.
5. To furnish such institutions of relief as hospitals, outdoor stations, etc.

How a sensible people could expect really to conduct a slave into freedom with less than this is hard to see. Of course even with such tutelage extending over a period of two or three decades the ultimate end had to be enfranchisement and political and social freedom for those freedmen who attained a certain set standard. Otherwise the whole training had neither object nor guarantee.

Naturally the Bureau was no sooner established than it faced implacable enemies. The white South naturally opposed to a man because it practically abolished private profit in the exploitation of labor. To step from slave to free labor was economic catastrophe in the opinion of the white South: but to step further to free labor organized primarily for the laborers' benefit, this not only was unthinkable for the white South but it even touched the economic sensibilities of the white North. Already the nation owed a staggering debt. It would not face any large increase for such a purpose. Moreover, who could conduct such an enterprise? It would have taxed in ordinary times the ability and self sacrifice of the nation to have found men in sufficient quantity who could and would have conducted honestly and efficiently such a tremendous experiment in human uplift. And these were not ordinary times.

Nevertheless a bureau had to be established at least temporarily as a clearing house for the numberless departments of the armies dealing with freedmen and holding land and property in their name.

As General Howard, the head of the Bureau said, this Bureau was really a government and partially ruled the South from the close of the war until 1870. "It made laws, executed them and interpreted them. It laid and collected taxes, defined and punished crime, maintained and used military force and dictated such measures as it thought necessary and proper for the accomplishment of its varied ends." Its establishment was a herculean task both physically and socially, and it accomplished a great work before it was repudiated. Carl Schurz in 1864 felt warranted in saying, "Not half of the labor that has been done in the South this year, or will be done there next year, would have been or would be done but for the exertions of the Freedmen's Bureau. . . No other agency, except one placed there by the national government, could have wielded the moral power whose interposition was so necessary to prevent the Southern society from falling at once into the chaos of a general collision between its different elements."[12]

The nation knew, however, that, the Freedmen's Bureau was temporary. What should follow it? The attitude of the South was not reassuring. Carl Schurz reported that: "Some planters held back their former slaves on their plantations by brute force. Armed bands of white men patrolled the country roads to drive back the Negroes wandering about. Dead bodies of murdered Negroes were found on and near the highways and by-paths. Gruesome reports came from the hospitals—reports of colored men and women whose ears had been cut off, whose skulls had been broken by blows, whose bodies had been slashed by knives or lacerated by scourges. A number of such cases I had occasion to examine myself. A veritable reign of terror prevailed in many parts of the South. The Negro found scant justice in the local courts against the white man. He could look for protection only to the military forces of the United States still garrisoning the 'states lately in rebellion' and to the Freedmen's Bureau."[14]

The determination to reconstruct the South without recognizing the Negro as a voter was manifest. The provisional governments set up by Lincoln and Johnson were based on white male suffrage. In Louisiana for instance, where free Negroes had wealth and prestige and had furnished thousands of soldiers under the proposed reconstruction and despite Lincoln's tactful suggestion—"Not one Negro was allowed to vote, though at that very time the wealthy, intelligent free colored people of the State paid taxes on property assessed at $15,000,000 and many of them were well known for their patriotic zeal and love for the Union. Thousands of colored men whose homes were in Louisiana served bravely in the national army and navy and many of the so-called Negroes in New Orleans could not be distinguished by the most intelligent strangers from the best class of white gentlemen either by color or manner, dress or language; still, as it was known by tradition and common fame that they were not of pure Caucasian descent, they could not vote."[13]

12. Report of Carl Schurz to President Johnson, in Senate Exec. Doc. No. 2, 39th Cong., 1st Sess.

13. Brewster, *Sketches of Southern Mystery, Treason and Murder,* p. 116.

Johnson feared this Southern program and like Lincoln suggested limited Negro suffrage. August 15th, 1865, he wrote to Governor Sharkey of Mississippi: "If you could extend the elective franchise to all persons of color who can read the Constitution of the United States in English and write their names, and to all persons of color who own real estate valued at not less than two hundred and fifty dollars, and pay taxes thereon, you would completely disarm the adversary and set an example the other states will follow. This you can do with perfect safety and you thus place the Southern States, in reference to free persons of color, upon the same basis with the free States. I hope and trust your convention will do this."[14]

The answer of the South to all such suggestions was the celebrated "Black Codes": "Alabama declared 'stubborn or refractory servants' or 'those who loiter away their time' to be 'vagrants' who could be hired out at compulsory service by law, while all Negro minors, far from being sent to school, were to be 'apprenticed' preferably to their father's former 'masters and mistresses.' In Florida it was decreed that no Negro could 'own, use or keep any bowie-knife, dirk, sword, firearms or ammunition of any kind' without a license from the Judge of Probate. In South Carolina the Legislature declared that 'no person of color shall pursue the practice of art, trade or business of an artisan, mechanic or shopkeeper or any other trade or employment besides that of husbandry or that of servant under contract for labor until he shall have obtained a license from the Judge of the District Court. Mississippi required that 'if a laborer shall quit the service of the employer before the expiration of his term of service without just cause, he shall forfeit his wages for that year.' Louisiana said that 'every adult freed man or woman shall furnish themselves with a comfortable home and visible means of support within twenty days after the passage of this act' and that any failing to do so should 'be immediately arrested', delivered to the court and 'hired out' by public advertisement, to some citizen, being the highest bidder, for the remainder year."[15]

These Codes were not reassuring to the friends of freedom. To be sure it was not a time to expect calm, cool, thoughtful action on the part of the South. Its economic condition was pitiable. Property in slaves to the extent perhaps of two thousand million dollars had suddenly

---

14. McPherson, *Reconstruction,* p. 19.
15. Atlanta University Publications, Atlanta, Ga., 1901, No. 6, p. 36.

disappeared. One thousand five hundred more millions representing the Confederate war debt, had largely disappeared. Large amounts of real estate and other property had been destroyed, industry had been disorganized, 250,000 men had been killed and many more maimed. With this went the moral effect of an unsuccessful war with all its letting down of social standards and quickening of hatred and discouragement—a situation which would make it difficult under any circumstances to reconstruct a new government and a new civilization. Moreover any human being of any color "doomed in his own person and his posterity to live without knowledge and without capacity to make anything his own and to toil that another may reap the fruits," is bound on sudden emancipation to loom like a great dread on the horizon.

The fear of Negro freedom in the South was increased by its own consciousness of guilt, yet it was reasonable to expect from it something more than mere repression and reaction toward slavery. To some small extent this expectation was fulfilled: the abolition of slavery was recognized and the civil rights of owning property and appearing as a witness in cases in which he was a party were generally granted the Negro; yet with these went such harsh regulations as largely neutralized the concessions and gave ground for the assumption that once free from Northern control the South would virtually re-enslave the Negro. The colored people themselves naturally feared this and protested, as in Mississippi, "against the reactionary policy prevailing and expressing the fear that the Legislature will pass such proscriptive laws as will drive the freedmen from the State or practically re-enslave them."[16]

As Professor Burgess (whom no one accuses of being Negrophile) says: "Almost every act, word or gesture of the Negro not consonant with good taste and good manners as well as good morals was made a crime or misdemeanor, for which he could first be fined by the magistrates and then be consigned to a condition of almost slavery for an indefinite time if he could not pay the bill."

All things considered, it seems probable that if the South had been permitted to have its way in 1865 the harshness of Negro slavery would have been mitigated so as to make slave trading difficult and to make it possible for a Negro to hold property if he got any and to appear in some cases in court; but that in most other respects the blacks would

16. October 7, 1865.

have remained in slavery. And no small number of whites even in the North were quite willing to contemplate such a solution.

In October, the democratic platform of Louisiana said "This is a government of white people," and although Johnson reported in December that Reconstruction was complete in North and South Carolina, Georgia, Alabama, Mississippi, Louisiana, Arkansas and Tennessee, yet everyone knew that the real problems of Reconstruction had just begun. The war caused by slavery could be stopped only by a real abolition of slavery.

It was as though the Germans invading France had found flocking to their camps the laboring forces of the invaded land, poor and destitute, but willing to work and willing to fight. What would have been the attitude of the successful invader when the war was ended? Gratitude alone counseled help for the Freedmen; wisdom counseled a real abolition of slavery; so far slavery had not been abolished in spite of the fact that the 13th Amendment proposed in February had been proclaimed in December. Freedom and citizenship were primarily a matter of state legislation; and emancipation from slavery was an economic problem—a question of work and wages, of land and capital—all these things were matters of state legislation. Unless then something was done to insure a proper legal status and legal protection for the Freedmen, the so-called abolition of slavery would be but a name. Furthermore there were grave political difficulties: According to the celebrated compromise in the Constitution, three-fifths of the slaves were counted in the Southern states as a basis of representation and this gave the white South as compared with the North a large political advantage. This advantage was now to be increased because, as freemen, the whole Negro population was to be counted and still the voting was confined to whites. The North, therefore, found themselves faced by the fact that the very people whom they had overcome in a costly and bloody war were now coming back with increased political power, with determination to keep just as much of slavery as they could and with freedom to act toward the nation that they had nearly destroyed, in whatever way the deep hatreds of a hurt and conquered people tempted them to act. All this was sinister and dangerous. Assume as large minded and forgiving an attitude as one could, either the abolition of slavery must be made real or the war was fought in vain.

The Negroes themselves naturally began to insist that without political power it was impossible to accomplish their economic freedom.

W.E.B. DU BOIS

Frederick Douglass said to President Johnson: "Your noble and humane predecessor placed in our hands the sword to assist in saving the nation and we do hope that you, his able successor, will favorably regard the placing in our hands the ballot with which to save ourselves." And when Johnson demurred on account of the hostility between blacks and poor whites, a committee of prominent colored men replied:

"Even if it were true, as you allege, that the hostility of the blacks toward the poor whites must necessarily project itself into a state of freedom, and that this enmity between the two races is even more intense in a state of freedom than in a state of slavery, in the name of heaven, we reverently ask, how can you, in view of your professed desire to promote the welfare of the black man, deprive him of all means of defense and clothe him, whom you regard as his enemy, in the panoply of political power?"[17]

Again as the Negro fugitive slave was already in camp before the nation was ready to receive him and was even trying to drive him back to his master; just as the Negro was already bearing arms before he was legally recognized as a soldier; so too he was voting before Negro suffrage was contemplated; to cite one instance at Davis Bend, Mississippi. "Early in 1865 a system was adopted for their government in which the freedmen took a considerable part. The Bend was divided into districts, each having a sheriff and judge appointed from among the more reliable and intelligent colored men. A general oversight of the proceedings was maintained by our officers in charge, who confirmed or modified the findings of the court. The shrewdness of the colored judges was very remarkable, though it was sometimes necessary to decrease the severity of the punishment they proposed. Fines and penal service on the Home Farm were the usual sentences they imposed. Petty theft and idleness were the most frequent causes of trouble, but my officers were able to report that exposed property was as safe on Davis Bend as it would be anywhere. The community distinctly demonstrated the capacity of the Negro to take care of himself and exercised under honest and competent direction the functions of self-government."[18]

Carl Schurz said in his celebrated report: "The emancipation of the slaves is submitted to only in so far as chattel slavery in the old form could not be kept up. But although the freedman is no longer

17. McPhenon, pp. 52, 56.
18. A. U. Publications, No. 12, p. 38; Cf. also Fleming, Vol. 1, p. 355.

considered the property of the individual master, he is considered the slave of society and all independent State legislation will share the tendency to make him such.

"The solution of the problem would be very much facilitated by enabling all the loyal and free labor elements in the South to exercise a healthy influence upon legislation. It will hardly be possible to secure the freedman against oppressive class legislation and private persecution unless he be endowed with a certain measure of political power."

To the argument of ignorance Schurz replied: "The effect of the extension of the franchise to the colored people upon the development of free labor and upon the security of human rights in the South being the principal object in view, the objections raised on the ground of the ignorance of the freedmen become unimportant. Practical liberty is a good school... It is idle to say that it will be time to speak of Negro suffrage when the whole colored race will be educated, for the ballot may be necessary to him to secure his education."[19]

Thus Negro suffrage was forced to the front, not as a method of humiliating the South; not as a theoretical and dangerous gift to the Freedmen; not according to any preconcerted plan but simply because of the grim necessities of the situation. The North must either give up the fruits of war, keep a Freedmen's Bureau for a generation or use the Negro vote to reconstruct the Southern states and to insure such legislation as would at least begin the economic emancipation of the slave.

In other words the North being unable to free the slave, let him try to free himself. And he did, and this was his greatest gift to this nation.

Let us return to the steps by which the Negro accomplished this task.

In 1866, the joint committee of Congress on Reconstruction said that in the South: "A large proportion of the population had become, instead of mere chattels, free men and citizens. Through all the past struggle these had remained true and loyal and had, in large numbers, fought on the side of the Union. It was impossible to abandon them without securing them their rights as free men and citizens. The whole civilized world would have cried out against such base ingratitude and the bare idea is offensive to all right thinking men. Hence it became important to inquire what could be done to secure their rights, civil and political."

---

19. Schurz' Report.

The report then proceeded to emphasize the increased political power of the South and recommended the Fourteenth Amendment, since: "It appeared to your committee that the rights of these persons by whom the basis of representation had been thus increased should be recognized by the General Government. While slaves, they were not considered as having any rights, civil or political. It did not seem just or proper that all the political advantages derived from their becoming free should be confined to their former masters who had fought against the Union and withheld from themselves who had always been loyal."[20]

Nor did there seem to be any hope that the South would voluntarily change its attitude within any reasonable time. As Carl Schurz wrote: "I deem it proper, however, to offer a few remarks on the assertion frequently put forth, that the franchise is likely to be extended to the colored man by the voluntary action of the southern whites themselves. My observation leads me to a contrary opinion. Aside from a very few enlightened men, I found but one class of people in favor of the enfranchisement of the blacks: it was the class of Unionists who found themselves politically ostracised and looked upon the enfranchisement of the loyal Negroes as the salvation of the whole loyal element. . . The masses are strongly opposed to colored suffrage; anybody that dares to advocate it is stigmatized as a dangerous fanatic."

"The only manner in which, in my opinion, the southern people can be induced to grant to the freedmen some measure of self-protecting power in the form of suffrage, is to make it a consideration precedent to 'readmission'."[21]

During 1866, the Freedmen's Bureau received over a million dollars mostly from the Freedmen's fund, sales of crop, rent of lands and buildings and school taxes. The chief expenditure was in wages, rent and schools. It was evident that the Negro was demanding education. Schools arose immediately among the refugees and Negro soldiers. They were helped by voluntary taxation of the Negroes and then by the activity of Northern religious bodies. Seldom in the history of the world has an almost totally illiterate population been given the means of self-education in so short a time. The movement started with the Negroes themselves and they continued to form the dynamic force behind it. "This great multitude arose up simultaneously and asked for

---

20. House Reports, No. 30, 39th Congress, 1st Session.
21. Schurz' Report.

intelligence." There can be no doubt that these schools were a great conservative steadying force to which the South owes much. It must not be forgotten that among the agents of the Freedmen's Bureau were not only soldiers and politicians but school teachers and educational leaders like Ware and Cravath.

In 1866, nearly 100,000 Negroes were in the schools under 1300 teachers and schools for Negroes had been opened in nearly all the southern states. A second Freedmen's Bureau act was passed extending the work of the Bureau, and the Freedmen's Bank which had been started in 1865 and had by 1866 twenty branches and $300,000 in savings.

Congress came to blows with President Johnson. His plan of reconstruction with white male suffrage was repudiated and the 14th Amendment was proposed by Congress which was designed to force the South to accept Negro suffrage on penalty of losing a proportionate amount of their representation in Congress. The 14th Amendment was long delayed and did not in fact become a law until July, 1868. Meantime, Congress adopted more drastic measures. By the Reconstruction Acts, the first of which passed March 2nd, the South was divided into five military districts, Negro suffrage was established for the constitutional conventions and the 14th Amendment made a prerequisite for readmission of states to the Union.

What was the result? No language has been spared to describe the results of Negro suffrage as the worst imaginable. Every effort of historical and social science and propaganda have supported this view; and its acceptance has been well nigh universal, because it was so clearly to the interests of the chief parties involved to forget their own shortcomings and put the blame on the Negro. As a colored man put it, they closed the "bloody chasm" but closed up the Negro inside. Yet, without Negro suffrage, slavery could not have been abolished in the United States and while there were bad results arising from the enfranchisement of the slaves as there necessarily had to be, the main results were not bad. Let us not forget that the white South believed it to be of vital interest to its welfare that the experiment of Negro suffrage should fail ignominiously and that almost to a man the whites were willing to insure this failure either by active force or passive resistance; that beside this there were, as might be expected in a day of social upheaval, men, white and black, Northern and Southern, only too eager to take advantage of such a situation for feathering their own nests. The results in such case had to be evil but to charge the evil to Negro suffrage is unfair. It may be charged to anger, poverty, venality and ignorance, but the anger and poverty were the almost inevitable aftermath of war; the venality was much more reprehensible as exhibited among whites than among Negroes, and while ignorance was the curse of the Negroes, the fault was not theirs and they took the initiative to correct it.

Negro suffrage was without doubt a tremendous experiment but with all its manifest failure it succeeded to an astounding degree; it made the immediate re-establishment of the old slavery impossible and it was probably the only quick method of doing this; it gave the Freedmen's sons a chance to begin their education. It diverted the energy of the white South from economic development to the recovery of political power and in this interval—small as it was—the Negro took his first steps toward economic freedom. It was the greatest and most important step toward world democracy of all men of all races ever taken in the modern world.

Let us see just what happened when the Negroes gained the right to vote, first in the conventions which reconstructed the form of government and afterward in the regular state governments. The continual charge is made that the South was put under Negro government—that ignorant exslaves ruled the land. This is untrue. Negroes did not dominate southern legislatures, and in only two states did they have a majority of the legislature at any time. In Alabama in the years of 1868–69 there were 106 whites and 27 Negroes in the legislature; in the year 1876 there were 104 whites and 29 Negroes. In Arkansas, 1868–69 there were 8 Negroes and 96 whites. In Georgia there were 186 whites and 33 Negroes. In Mississippi, 1870–1, there were 106 whites and 34 Negroes and in 1876, 132 whites and 21 Negroes. In North Carolina, 149 whites and 21 Negroes; in South Carolina 1868–69, 72 whites and 85 Negroes and in 1876, 70 whites and 54 Negroes. In Texas, 1870–71 there were no whites and 10 Negroes. In Virginia, 1868–69, 119 whites and 18 Negroes and in 1876, 112 whites and 13 Negroes.[22]

"Statistics show, however, that with the exception of South Carolina and Mississippi, no state and not even any department of a state government was ever dominated altogether by Negroes. The Negroes never wanted and never had complete control in the Southern states.

22. *Journal of Negro History*, Vol. 5, p. 238.

The most important offices were generally held by white men. Only two Negroes ever served in the United States Senate, Hiram R. Revells and B. K. Bruce; and only twenty ever became representatives in the House and all these did not serve at the same time, although some of them were elected for more than one term."[23]

The Negroes who held office, held for the most part minor offices and most of them were ignorant men. Some of them were venal and vicious but this was not true in all cases. Indeed the Freedmen were pathetic too in their attempt to choose the best persons but they were singularly limited in their choice. Their former white masters were either disfranchised or bitterly hostile or ready to deceive them. The "carpet-baggers" often cheated them; their own ranks had few men of experience and training. Yet some of the colored men who served them well deserve special mention:

Samuel J. Lee, a member of the South Carolina legislature, was considered by the whites as one of the best criminal lawyers of the state. When he died local courts were adjourned and the whole city mourned. Bishop Isaac Clinton who served as Treasurer of Orangeburg, S. C. for eight years was held in highest esteem by his white neighbors and upon the occasion of his death business was suspended as a mark of respect. In certain communities Negroes were retained in office for years after the restoration of Democratic party control as, for example Mr. George Harriot in Georgetown, S. C. who was Superintendent of Education for the county. Beaufort, South Carolina, retained Negroes as sheriffs and school officials.

J. T. White who was Commissioner of Public Works and Internal Improvements in Arkansas; M. W. Gibbs who was Municipal Judge in Little Rock, and J. C. Corbin, who was State Superintendent of Schools in Arkansas, had creditable records.[24] John R. Lynch, when speaker of Mississippi House of Representatives, was given a public testimonial by Republicans and Democrats and the leading Democratic paper said: "His bearing in office had been so proper and his rulings in such marked contrast to the partisan conduct of the ignoble whites of his party who have aspired to be leaders of the blacks, that the conservatives cheerfully joined in the testimonial."[25]

---

23. *Journal of Negro History,* Vol. 7, pp. 127ff.

24. *Journal of Negro History,* Vol. 7, p. 424.

25. Jackson, Miss., *Clarion,* April 24, 1873.

Of the colored treasurer of South Carolina, Governor Chamberlain said: "I have never heard one word or seen one act of Mr. Cardoza's which did not confirm my confidence in his personal integrity and his political honor and zeal for the honest administration of the State Government. On every occasion and under all circumstances he has been against fraud and jobbery and in favor of good measures and good men."[26]

Jonathan C. Gibbs, a colored man and the first State Superintendent of Instructions in Florida, was a graduate of Dartmouth. He established the system and brought it to success, dying in harness in 1874. The first Negro graduate of Harvard College served in South Carolina, before he became chief executive officer of the association that erected the Grant's Tomb in New York.

In Louisiana we may mention Acting-Governor Pinchback, and Lieutenant-Governor Dunn, and Treasurer Dubuclet who was investigated by United States officials. E. P. White, afterward Chief Justice of the United States, reported that his funds had been honestly handled. Such men—and there were others—ought not to be forgotten or confounded with other types of colored and white Reconstruction leaders.

Between 1871 and 1901, twenty-two Negroes sat in Congress—two as senators and twenty as representatives; three or four others were undoubtedly elected but were not seated. Ten of these twenty-two Negroes were college bred: Cain of South Carolina was trained at Wilberforce and afterward became bishop of the African Methodist Church; Revels was educated at Knox College, Illinois, or at a Quaker Seminary, in Indiana; Cheatham was a graduate of Shaw; Murray was trained at the University of South Carolina; Langston was a graduate of Oberlin; five others were lawyers of whom the most brilliant was Robert Brown Elliott; he was a graduate of Eton College, England; Rapier was educated in Canada and O'Hara studied at Howard University; Miller graduated from Lincoln and White from Howard University. The other twelve men were self-taught: one was a thriving merchant tailor, one a barber, three were farmers, one a photographer, one a pilot and one a merchant.[27]

---

26. Walter Allen, *Governor Chamberlain's Administration in South Carolina,* New York, 1888, p. 82.

27. *Journal of Negro History,* Vol. 7, pp. 127ff.

Of those who served in the Senate, one served an unexpired term and the other six years. In the House, one representative served one term from Virginia. From North Carolina one served one term and two, two terms. Georgia was represented by a Negro for one term and Mississippi for two terms. South Carolina had eight representatives, two of them served five terms, three two terms, and the rest one term. Beside these there were other Negro office holders who were fully the peers of white men; and those without formal training in the schools were in many cases men of unusual force and native ability.

James G. Blaine who served with nearly all these men approved of sending them to Congress: "If it is to be viewed simply as an experiment, it was triumphantly successful. The colored men who took seats in both Senate and House did not appear ignorant or helpless. They were as a rule studious, earnest, ambitious men whose public conduct—as illustrated by Mr. Revels and Mr. Bruce in the Senate and by Mr. Rapier, Mr. Lynch and Mr. Rainey in the House would be honorable to any race. Coals of fire were heaped on the heads of all their enemies when the colored men in Congress heartily joined in removing the disabilities of those who had before been their oppressors, and who, with deep regret be it said, have continued to treat them with injustice and ignominy."[28]

He cites the magnanimity of Senator Rainey: "When the Amnesty Bill came before the House for consideration, Mr. Rainey of South Carolina, speaking for the colored race whom he represented said: 'It is not the disposition of my constituents that these disabilities should longer be retained. We are desirous of being magnanimous; it may be that we are so to a fault. Nevertheless we have open and frank hearts towards those who were our oppressors and taskmasters. We foster no enmity now, and we desire to foster none, for their acts in the past to us or to the Government we love so well. But while we are willing to accord them their enfranchisement and here today give our votes that they may be amnestied, while we declare our hearts open and free from any vindictive feelings toward them, we would say to those gentlemen on the other side that there is another class of citizens in the country who have certain rights and immunities which they would like you, sirs, to remember and respect. . . We invoke you gentlemen, to show the same kindly feeling towards us, a race long oppressed, and

---

28. Blaine, *Twenty Years in Congress,* Vol. 2, p. 515.

in demonstration of this humane and just feeling, I implore you, give support to the Civil Rights Bill, which we have been asking at your hands, lo! these many days."[29]

The chief charge against Negro governments has to do with property. These governments are charged with attacking property and the charge is true. This, although not perhaps sensed at the time, was their real reason for being. The exslaves must have land and capital or they would fall back into slavery. The masters had both; there must be a transfer. It was at first proposed that land be confiscated in the South and given to the Freedmen. "Forty Acres and a Mule" was the widespread promise made several times with official sanction. This was perhaps the least that the United States Government could have done to insure emancipation, but such a program would have cost money. In the early anger of the war, it seemed to many fair to confiscate land for this purpose without payment and some land was thus sequestered. But manifestly with all the losses of war and with the loss of the slaves it was unfair to take the land of the South without some compensation. The North was unwilling to add to its tremendous debt anything further to insure the economic independence of the Freedmen. The Freedmen therefore themselves with their political power and with such economic advantage as the war gave them, tried to get hold of land.

The Negro party platform of 1876, in one state, advocated "division of lands of the state as far as practical into small farms in order that the masses of our people may be enabled to become landholders." In the Constitutional Convention of South Carolina, a colored man said: "One of the greatest of slavery bulwarks was the infernal plantation system, one man owning his thousand, another his twenty, another fifty thousands acres of land. This is the only way by which we will break up that system, and I maintain that our freedom will be of no effect if we allow it to continue. What is the main cause of the prosperity of the North. It is because every man has his own farm and is free and independent. Let the lands of the South be similarly divided. I would not say for one moment they should be confiscated but if sold to maintain the war, now that slavery is destroyed, let the plantation system go with it. We will never have true freedom until we abolish the system of agriculture which existed in the Southern States. It is useless to have any schools while we maintain the stronghold of slavery as the

---

29. Blaine, *Twenty Years in Congress,* pp. 513–14.

agricultural system of the country."[30] This question kept coming up in the South Carolina convention and elsewhere. Such arguments led in South Carolina to a scheme to buy land and distribute it and some $800,000 was appropriated for this purpose.

In the second place, property was attacked through the tax system. The South had been terribly impoverished and was saddled with new social burdens. Many of the things which had been done well or indifferently by the plantations—like the punishment of crime and the care of the sick and the insane, and such schooling as there was, with most other matters of social uplift were, after the war, transferred to the control of the state. Moreover the few and comparatively indifferent public buildings of slavery days had been ruined either by actual warfare or by neglect. Thus a new and tremendous burden of social taxation was put upon the reconstructed states.

As a southern writer says of the state of Mississippi: "The work of restoration which the government was obliged to undertake, made increased expenses necessary. During the period of the war, and for several years thereafter, public buildings and state institutions were permitted to fall into decay. The state house and grounds, the executive mansion, the penitentiary, the insane asylum, and the buildings for the blind, deaf and dumb, were in a dilapidated condition and had to be extended and repaired. A new building for the blind was purchased and fitted up. The reconstructionists established a public school system and spent money to maintain and support it, perhaps too freely, in view of the impoverishment of the people. When they took hold, warrants were worth but sixty or seventy cents on the dollar, a fact which made the price of building materials used in the work of construction correspondingly higher."[31]

In addition to all this there was fraud and stealing. There were white men who cheated and secured large sums. Most of $800,000 appropriated for land in South Carolina was wasted in graft. Bills for wine and furniture in South Carolina were enormous; the printing bill of Mississippi was ridiculously extravagant. Colored men shared in this loot but they at least had some excuse. We may not forget that among slaves stealing is not the crime that it becomes in free industry. The slave is victim of a theft so hateful that nothing he can steal can ever match it. The freedmen of 1868 still shared the slave psychology. The

---

30. Fleming, Vol. 1, pp. 450–1.

31. J. W. Garner, *Reconstruction in Mississippi*, New York, 1901, p. 322.

larger part of the stealing was done by white men—Northerners and Southerners—and we must remember that it was not the first time that there had been stealing and corruption in the South and that the whole moral tone of the nation had been ruined by war. For instance:

In 1839 it was reported in Mississippi that ninety per cent of the fines collected by sheriffs and clerks were unaccounted for. In 1841 the State Treasurer acknowledged himself "at a loss to determine the precise liabilities of the state and her means of paying the same." And in 1839 the auditor's books had not been posted for eighteen months, no entries made for a year, and no vouchers examined for three years. Congress gave Jefferson College, Natchez, more than 46,000 acres of land; before the war this whole property had "disappeared" and the college was closed. Congress gave to Mississippi among other states, the "16th section" of the public lands for schools. In thirty years the proceeds of this land in Mississippi were embezzled to the amount of at least one and a half millions of dollars. In Columbus, Mississippi a receiver of public monies stole $100,000 and resigned. His successor stole $55,000 and a treasury agent wrote: "Another receiver would probably follow in the footsteps of the two. You will not be surprised if I recommend him being retained in preference to another appointment." From 1830 to 1860 southern men in federal offices alone embezzled more than a million dollars—a far greater sum then than now.

There might have been less stealing in the South during Reconstruction without Negro suffrage but it is certainly highly instructive to remember that the mark of the thief which dragged its slime across nearly every great Northern State and almost up to the presidential chair could not certainly in those cases be charged against the vote of black men. This was the day when a national Secretary of War was caught stealing, a vice president presumably took bribes, a private secretary of the president, a chief clerk of the Treasury, and eighty-six government officials stole millions in the Whiskey frauds; while the "Credit Mobilier" filched millions and bribed the government to an extent never fully revealed; not to mention less distinguished thieves like Tweed.

Is it surprising that in such an atmosphere a new race learning the a-b-c of government should have become the tools of thieves? And when they did, was the stealing their fault or was it justly chargeable to their enfranchisement? Then too, a careful examination of the alleged stealing in the South reveals much: First, there is repeated exaggeration.

For instance, it is said that the taxation in Mississippi was fourteen times as great in 1874 as in 1869. This sounds staggering until we learn that the State taxation in 1869 was only ten cents on one hundred dollars and that the expenses of government in 1874 were only twice as great as in 1860 and that too with a depreciated currency. It could certainly be argued that the State government in Mississippi was doing enough additional work in 1874 to warrant greatly increased cost. The character of much of the stealing shows who were the thieves. The frauds through the manipulation of State and railway bonds and of bank notes must have inured chiefly to the benefit of experienced white men and this must have been largely the case in the furnishing and printing frauds. It was chiefly in the extravagance for "sundries and incidentals" and direct money payments for votes that the Negroes received their share. The character of the real thieving shows that white men must have been the chief beneficiaries and that as a former South Carolina slaveholder said:

"The legislature, ignorant as it is, could not have been bribed without money; that must have been furnished from some source that it is our duty to discover. A legislature composed chiefly of our former slaves has been bribed. One prominent feature of this transaction is the part which native Carolinians have played in it, some of our own household men whom the State, in the past, has delighted to honor, appealing to their cupidity and avarice make them the instruments to effect the robbery of their impoverished white brethren. Our former slaves have been bribed by these men to give them the privilege by law of plundering the property holders of the state."[32]

Even those who mocked and sneered at Negro legislators brought now and then words of praise: "But beneath all this shocking burlesque upon Legislative proceedings we must not forget that there is something very real to this uncouth and untutored multitude. It is not all shame, not all burlesque. They have a genuine interest and a genuine earnestness in the business of the assembly which we are bound to recognize and respect. . . They have an earnest purpose, born of conviction that their conditions are not fully assured, which lends a sort of dignity to their proceedings. The barbarous, animated jargon in which they so often indulge is on occasion seen to be so transparently sincere and weighty in their own minds that sympathy supplants disgust. The whole thing is a wonderful novelty to them as well as to observers. Seven years ago these

32. Warley in *Brewster's Sketches,* p. 150.

men were raising corn and cotton under the whip of the overseer. Today they are raising points of order and questions of privilege. They find they can raise one as well as the other. They prefer the latter. It is easier and better paid. Then, it is the evidence of an accomplished result. It means escape and defence from old oppressors. It means liberty. It means the destruction of prison walls only too real to them. It is the sunshine of their lives. It is their day of jubilee. It is their long promised vision of the Lord God Almighty."[33]

But with the memory of the Freedmen's Bank before it, America should utter no sound as to Negro dishonesty during reconstruction. Here from the entrenched philanthropy of America with some of the greatest names of the day like Peter Cooper, William Cullen Bryant, Simon P. Chase, A. A. Low, Gerritt Smith, John Jay, A. S. Barnes, S. G. Howe, George L. Stearns, Edward Atkinson, Levi Coffin and others, a splendid scheme was launched to help the Freedmen save their pittance and encourage thrift and hope. On the covers of the pass books is said: "This is a benevolent institution and profits go to the depositors or to educational purposes for the Freedmen and their descendants. The whole institution is under the charter of Congress and receives the commendation of the President, Abraham Lincoln." With blare of trumpet it was chartered March 3rd, 1865; it collapsed in hopeless bankruptcy in 1873. It had received fifty-six millions of dollars in deposits and failed owing over three millions most of which was never repaid. A committee of Congress composed of both Democrats and Republicans said in 1876:

"The law lent no efficacy to the moral obligations assumed by the trustees, officers, and agents and the whole concern inevitably became as a 'whited sepulchre' . . . The inspectors. . . were of little or no value, either through the connivance and ignorance of the inspectors or the indifference of the trustees to their reports. . . The committe of examination. . . were still more careless and inefficient, while the board of trustees, as a supervising and administrative body, intrusted with the fullest power of general control over the management, proved utterly faithless to the trust reposed in them. . .

"The depositors were of small account now compared with the personal interest of the political jobbers, real estate pools, and

---

33. A Liberal Republican's description of the S. C. Legislature in 1871, Fleming, Vol. 2, pp. 53–4.

fancy-stock speculators, who were organizing a raid upon the Freedmen's money and resorted to. . . amendment of the charter to facilitate their operations. . . This mass of putridity, the District government, now abhorred of all men, and abandoned and repudiated even by the political authors of its being, was represented in the bank by no less than five of its high officers. . . all of whom were in one way or other concerned in speculations involving a free use of the funds of the Freedmen's Bank. They were high in power, too, with the dominant influence in Congress, as the legislation they asked or sanctioned and obtained, fully demonstrated. Thus it was that without consulting the wishes or regarding the interests of those most concerned—the depositors—the vaults of the bank were literally thrown open to unscrupulous greed and rapacity. The toilsome savings of the poor Negroes hoarded and laid by for a rainy day, through the carelessness and dishonest connivance of their self-constituted guardians, melted away. . ."[34]

Even in bankruptcy the institution was not allowed to come under the operation of the ordinary laws but was liquidated and protected by a special law, the liquidators picking its corpse and the helpless victims being finally robbed not only of their money but of much of their faith in white folk.

Let us laugh hilariously if we must over the golden spittoons of South Carolina but let us also remember that at most the freedmen filched bits from those who had all and not all from those who had nothing; and that the black man had at least the saving grace to hide his petty theft by enshrining the nasty American habit of spitting in the sheen of sunshine.

With all these difficulties and failings, what did the Freedmen in politics during the critical years of their first investment with the suffrage accomplish? We may recognize three things which Negro rule gave to the South:

1. Democratic government.
2. Free public schools.
3. New social legislation.

Two states will illustrate conditions of government in the South before and after Negro rule. In South Carolina there was before the

---

34. Fleming, Vol. 1, pp. 382ff.

W.E.B. DU BOIS

war a property qualification for office holders, and in part, for voters. The Constitution of 1868, on the other hand, was a modern democratic document starting (in marked contrast to the old constitution) with a declaration that "We, the People,"[35] framed it and preceded by a broad Declaration of Rights which did away with property qualifications and based representation directly on population instead of property. It especially took up new subjects of social legislation, declaring navigable rivers free public highways, instituting homestead exemptions, establishing boards of county commissioners, providing for a new penal code of laws, establishing universal manhood suffrage "without distinction of race or color," devoting six sections to charitable and penal institutions and six to corporations, providing separate property for married women, etc. Above all, eleven sections of the Tenth Article were devoted to the establishment of a complete public school system.

So satisfactory was the constitution thus adopted by Negro suffrage and by a convention composed of a majority of blacks that the States lived twenty-seven years under it without essential change and when the constitution was revised in 1895, the revision was practically nothing more than an amplification of the Constitution of 1868. No essential advance step of the former document was changed except the suffrage article to disfranchise Negroes.

In Mississippi the Constitution of 1868 was, as compared with that before the war, more democratic. It not only forbade distinctions on account of color but abolished all property qualifications for jury service and property and educational qualifications for suffrage; it required less rigorous qualifications for office; it prohibited the lending of the credit of the State for private corporations—an abuse dating back as far as 1830. It increased the powers of the governor, raised the low State salaries, and increased the number of state officials. New ideas like the public school system and the immigration bureau were introduced and in general the activity of the State greatly and necessarily enlarged. Finally that was the only constitution of the State ever submitted to popular approval at the polls. This constitution remained in force twenty-two years.

In general the words of Judge Albion W. Tourgee, "a carpet-bagger," are true when he says of the Negro governments: "They obeyed the Constitution of the United States and annulled the bonds of states,

---

35. Some of the Reconstruction Constitutions preceding Negro Suffrage showed tendencies toward democratization among the whites.

counties and cities which had been issued to carry on the war of rebellion and maintain armies in the field against the Union. They instituted a public school system in a realm where public schools had been unknown. They opened the ballot box and jury box to thousands of white men who had been debarred from them by a lack of earthly possessions. They introduced home rule in the South. They abolished the whipping post, the branding iron, the stocks and other barbarous forms of punishment which had up to that time prevailed. They reduced capital felonies from about twenty to two or three. In an age of extravagance they were extravagant in the sums appropriated for public works. In all of that time no man's rights of person were invaded under the forms of law. Every Democrat's life, home, fireside and business were safe. No man obstructed any white man's way to the ballot box, interfered with his freedom of speech or boycotted him, on account of his political faith."[36]

A thorough study of the legislation accompanying these constitutions and its changes since would, of course, be necessary before a full picture of the situation could be given. This has not been done but so far as my studies have gone I have been surprised at the comparatively small amount of change in law and government which the overthrow of Negro rule brought about. There were sharp and often hurtful economies introduced, marking the return of property to power, there was a sweeping change in officials but the main body of Reconstruction legislation stood.

There is no doubt but that the thirst of the black man for knowledge—a thirst which has been too persistent and durable to be mere curiosity or whim—gave birth to the public free school system of the South. It was the question upon which the black voters and legislators insisted more than anything else and while it is possible to find some vestiges of free schools in some of the Southern States before the war yet a universal, well established system dates from the day that the black man got political power. Common school instruction in the South, in the modern sense of the term, was begun for Negroes by the Freedmen's Bureau and missionary societies, and the State public school systems for all children were formed mainly by Negro Reconstruction governments.

The earlier state constitutions of Mississippi "from 1817 to 1864 contained a declaration that 'Religion, morality and knowledge being

---

36. Chicago Weekly *Inter-Ocean*, Dec. 26, 1890.

necessary to good government, the preservation of liberty and the happiness of mankind, schools and the means of education shall forever be encouraged.' It was not, however, until 1868 that encouragement was given to any general system of public schools meant to embrace the whole youthful population." The Constitution of 1868 makes it the duty of the legislature to establish "a uniform system of free public schools by taxation or otherwise for all children between the ages of five and twenty-one years." In Alabama the Reconstruction Constiution of 1868 provided that "It shall be the duty of the Board of Education to establish throughout the State in each township or other school district which it may have created, one or more schools at which all children of the state between the ages of five and twenty-one years may attend free of charge." Arkansas in 1868, Florida in 1869, Virginia in 1870, established school systems. The Constitution of 1868 in Louisiana required the general assembly to establish "at least one free public school in every parish," and that these schools should make no "distinction of race, color or previous condition." Georgia's system was not fully established until 1873.

We are apt to forget that in all human probability the granting of Negro manhood suffrage was decisive in rendering permanent the foundation of the Negro common school. Even after the overthrow of the Negro governments, if the Negroes had been left a servile caste, personally free but politically powerless, it is not reasonable to think that a system of common schools would have been provided for them by the Southern states. Serfdom and education have ever proven contradictory terms. But when Congress, backed by the nation, determined to make the Negroes full-fledged voting citizens, the South had a hard dilemma before her; either to keep the Negroes under as an ignorant proletariat and stand the chance of being ruled eventually from the slums and jails, or to join in helping to raise these wards of the nation to a position of intelligence and thrift by means of a public school system.[37]

The "carpet-bag" governments hastened the decision of the South and although there was a period of hesitation and retrogression after the overthrow of Negro rule in the early seventies, yet the South saw that to abolish Negro schools in addition to nullifying the Negro vote would invite Northern interference; and thus eventually every Southern state confirmed the work of the Negro legislators and maintained the Negro public schools along with the white.

---

37. Cf. Atlanta University Pub. No. 6 and No. 16.

Finally, in legislation covering property the wider functions of the State, the punishment of crime and the like, it is sufficient to say that the laws on these points established by Reconstruction legislatures were not only different and even revolutionary to the laws of the older South, but they were so wise and so well suited to the needs of the new South that in spite of a retrogressive movement following the overthrow of the Negro governments, the mass of this legislation with elaboration and development still stands on the statute books of the South.

Reconstruction constitutions, practically unaltered, were kept in

Florida, 1868–1885	17 years
Virginia, 1870–1902........................	32 years
South Carolina, 1868–1895	27 years
Mississippi, 1868–1890	22 years

Even in the case of states like Alabama, Georgia, North Carolina and Louisiana, which adopted new constitutions to signify the overthrow of Negro rule, the new constitutions are nearer the model of the Reconstruction document than they are to the previous constitutions. They differ from the Negro constitutions in minor details but very little in general conception.

Here then on the whole was a much more favorable result of a great experiment in democracy than the world had a right to await. But even on its more sinister side and in the matter of the ignorance of inexperience and venality of the colored voters there came signs of better things. The theory of democratic government is not that the will of the people is always right, but rather that normal human beings of average intelligence will, if given a chance, learn the right and best course by bitter experience. This is precisely what the Negro voters showed indubitable signs of doing. First, they strove for schools to abolish their ignorance, and second, a large and growing number of them revolted against the carnival of extravagance and stealing that marred the beginning of Reconstruction and joined with the best elements to institute reform; and the greatest stigma on the white South is not that it opposed Negro suffrage and resented theft and incompetence, but that when it saw the reform movement growing and even in some cases triumphing, and a larger and larger number of black voters learning to vote for honesty and ability, it still preferred a Reign of Terror to a campaign of education and disfranchised Negroes instead of punishing rascals.

No one has expressed this more convincingly than a Negro who was himself a member of the Reconstruction legislature of South Carolina and who spoke at the convention which disfranchised him, against one of the onslaughts of Tillman:

"The gentleman from Edgefield (Mr. Tillman) speaks of the piling up of the State debt; of jobbery and speculation during the period between 1869 and 1873 in South Carolina, but he has not found voice eloquent enough nor pen exact enough to mention those imperishable gifts bestowed upon South Carolina between 1873 and 1876 by Negro legislators—the laws relative to finance, the building of penal and charitable institutions and, greatest of all, the establishment of the public school system. Starting as infants in legislation in 1869, many wise measures were not thought of, many injudicious acts were passed. But in the administration of affairs for the next four years, having learned by experience the result of bad acts, we immediately passed reformatory laws touching every department of state, county, municipal and town governments. These enactments are today upon the statute books of South Carolina. They stand as living witnesses of the Negro's fitness to vote and legislate upon the rights of mankind.

"When we came into power, town governments could lend the credit of their respective towns to secure funds at any rate of interest that the council saw fit to pay. Some of the towns paid as high as twenty percent. We passed an act prohibiting town governments from pledging the credit of their hamlets for money bearing a greater rate of interest than five percent.

"Up to 1874, inclusive, the State Treasurer had the power to pay out State funds as he pleased. He could elect whether he would pay out the funds on appropriations that would place the money in the hands of the speculators, or would apply them to appropriations that were honest and necessary. We saw the evil of this and passed an act making specific levies and collections of taxes for specific appropriations.

"Another source of profligacy in the expenditure of funds was the law that provided for and empowered the levying and collecting of special taxes by school districts, in the name of the schools. We saw its evil and by a Constitutional amendment provided that there should only be levied and collected annually a tax of two mills for school purposes, and took away from the school districts the power to levy and to collect taxes of any kind. By this act we cured the evils that had been inflicted upon us in the name of the schools, settled the public school question for all time to come and established the system upon an honest financial basis.

"Next, we learned during the period from 1869 to 1874 inclusive, that what was denominated the floating indebtedness, covering the printing schemes and other indefinite expenditures, amounted to nearly $2,000,000. A conference was called of the leading Negro representatives in the two Houses together with the State Treasurer, also a Negro. After this conference we passed an act for the purpose of ascertaining the bona fide floating debt and found that it did not amount to more than $250,000 for the four years; we created a commission to sift that indebtedness and to scale it. Hence when the Democratic party came into power they found the floating debt covering the legislative and all other expenditures, fixed at the certain sum of $250,000. This same class of Negro legislators, led by the State Treasurer, Mr. F. L. Cardoza, knowing that there were millions of fraudulent bonds charged against the credit of the State, passed another act to ascertain the true bonded indebtedness and to provide for its settlement. Under this law, at one sweep, those entrusted with the power to do so, through Negro legislators, stamped six millions of bonds, denominated as conversion bonds, 'fraudulent.' The commission did not finish its work before 1876. In that year when the Hampton government came into power, there were still to be examined into and settled under the terms of the act passed by us and providing for the legitimate bonded indebtedness of the State, a little over two and a half million dollars worth of bonds and coupons which had not been passed upon.

"Governor Hampton, General Hagood, Judge Simonton, Judge Wallace and in fact, all of the conservative thinking Democrats aligned themselves under the provision enacted by us for the certain and final settlement of the bonded indebtedness and appealed to their Democratic legislators to stand by the Republican legislation on the subject and to confirm it. A faction in the Democratic party obtained a majority of the Democrats in the legislature against settling the question and they endeavored to open up anew the whole subject of the State debt. We had a little over thirty members in the House and enough Republican senators to sustain the Hampton conservative faction and to stand up for honest finance, or by our votes to place the debt question of the old State into the hands of the plunderers and speculators. We were appealed to by General Hagood, through me, and my answer to him was in these words: 'General, our people have learned the difference between profligate and honest legislation. We have passed acts of financial reform, and with the assistance of God, when the vote shall have been taken, you will be able to record for the thirty-odd Negroes, slandered though they have been through the press, that they voted solidly with you all for the honest legislation and the preservation of the credit of the State.' The thirty-odd Negroes in the legislature and their senators by their votes did settle the debt question and saved the State $13,000,000.

"We were eight years in power. We had built school houses, established charitable institutions, built and maintained the penitentiary system, provided for the education of the deaf and dumb, rebuilt the jails and court houses, rebuilt the bridges and re-established the ferries. In short, we had reconstructed the State and placed it upon the road to prosperity and, at the same time, by our acts of financial reform, transmitted to the Hampton government an indebtedness not greater by more than $2,500,000 than was the bonded debt of the State in 1868, before the Republican Negroes and their white allies came into power."[38]

So too in Louisiana in 1872 and in Mississippi later the better element of the Republicans triumphed at the polls and joining with the Democrats instituted reforms, repudiated the worst extravagances and started toward better things. But unfortunately there was one thing that the white South feared more than Negro dishonesty, ignorance and incompetency, and that was Negro honesty, knowledge and efficiency.

Paint the "carpet-bag" governments and Negro rule as black as may be, the fact remains that the essence of the revolution which the overturning of the Negro governments made was to put these black men and their friends out of power. Outside the curtailing of expenses and stopping of extravagance, not only did their successors make few changes in the work which these legislatures and conventions had done, but they largely carried out their plans, followed their suggestions and strengthened their institutions. Practically the whole new growth of the South has been accomplished under laws which

---

38. This speech was made in the South Carolina Constitutional Convention of 1890 which disfranchised the Negro, by the Hon. Thomas E. Miller, ex-congressman and one of the six Negro members of the Convention. The Convention did not have the courage to publish it in their proceedings but it may be found in the Occasional Papers of the American Negro Academy No. 6, pp. 11–13.

black men helped to frame thirty years ago. I know of no greater compliment to Negro suffrage, and no greater contribution to real American democracy.[39]

The counter revolution came but it was too late. The Negro had stepped so far into new economic freedom that he could never be put back into slavery; and he had widened democracy to include not only a goodly and increasing number of his own group but the mass of the poor white South. The economic results of Negro suffrage were so great during the years from 1865 to 1876 that they have never been overthrown. The Freedmen's Bureau came virtually to an end in 1869. General Howard's report of that year said: "In spite of all disorders that have prevailed and the misfortunes that have fallen upon many parts of the South, a good degree of prosperity and success has already been attained. To the oft-repeated slander that the Negroes will not work and are incapable of taking care of themselves, it is a sufficient answer that their voluntary labor has produced nearly all the food that supported the whole people, besides a large amount of rice, sugar and tobacco for export, and two millions of bales of cotton each year, on which was paid into the United States Treasury during the years 1866 to 1867 a tax of more than forty millions of dollars ($40,000,000). It is not claimed that this result was wholly due to the care and oversight of this Bureau but it is safe to say as it has been said repeatedly by intelligent Southern white men, that without the Bureau or some similar agency, the material interests of the country would have greatly suffered and the government would have lost a far greater amount than has been expended in its maintenance. . .

"Of the nearly eight hundred thousand (800,000) acres of farming land and about five thousand (5,000) pieces of town property transferred to this Bureau by military and treasury officers, or taken up by assistant commissioners, enough was leased to produce a revenue of nearly four hundred thousand dollars ($400,000). Some farms were set apart in each state as homes for the destitute and helpless and a portion was cultivated by freedmen prior to its restoration. . .

"Notice the appropriations by Congress:

---

39. Cf. W. E. B. Du Bois, *Reconstruction* (American Historical Review, XV, No. 4, p. 871).

W. E. B. Du Bois, *Economics of Negro Emancipation* (Sociological Review, Oct., 1911, p. 303).

For the year ending July 1st, 1867	$6,940,450.00
For the year ending July 1st, 1868	3,936,300.00
For the relief of the destitute citizens in District of Columbia	40,000.00
For relief of destitute freedmen in the same	15,000.00
For expenses of paying bounties in 1869	214,000.00
For expenses for famine in Southern states and transportation.	1,865,645.00
For support of hospitals.	50,000.00
Making a total received from all sources of	$12,961,395.00

"Our expenditures from the beginning (including assumed accounts of the 'Department of Negro Affairs' from January 1st, 1865, to August 31, 1869) have been eleven million two hundred and forty-nine thousand and twenty-eight dollars and ten cents ($11,249,028.10). In addition to this cash expenditure the subsistence, medical supplies, quartermasters stores, issued to the refugees and freedmen prior to July 1st, 1866, were furnished by the commissary, medical and quartermasters department, and accounted for in the current expenses of those departments; they were not charged to nor paid for by my officers. They amounted to two million three hundred and thirty thousand seven hundred and eighty-eight dollars and seventy-two cents ($2,330,788.72) in original cost; but a large portion of these stores being damaged and condemned as unfit for issue to troops, their real value to the Government was probably less than one million dollars ($1,000,000). Adding their original cost to the amount expended from appropriations and other sources, the total expenses of our Government for refugees and freedmen to August 31, 1869, have been thirteen million five hundred and seventy-nine thousand eight hundred and sixteen dollars and eighty-two cents ($13,579,816.82). And deducting fifty thousand dollars ($50,000) set apart as a special relief fund for all classes of destitute people in the Southern states, the real cost has been thirteen million twenty-nine thousand eight hundred and sixteen dollars and eighty-two cents ($13,029,816.82)."[40]

By 1875, Negroes owned not less than 2,000,000 and perhaps as much as 4,000,000 acres of land and by 1880 this had increased to 6,000,000.

---

40. O. O. Howard, *Autobiography*, New York, 1907, Vol. 2, pp. 361–7, 371–2.

Notwithstanding the great step forward that the Negro had made this sinister fact faced him and his friends: he formed a minority of the population of the South. If that population was solidly arrayed against him his legal status was in danger and his economic progress was going to be difficult. It has been repeatedly charged that the action of the Negro solidified Southern opposition; and that the Negro refusing to listen to and make fair terms with his white neighbors, sought solely Northern alliance and the protection of Northern bayonets. This is not true and is turning facts hindside before. The ones who did the choosing were the Southern master class. When they got practically their full political rights in 1872 they had a chance to choose, if they would, the best of the Negroes as their allies and to work with them as against the most ruthless elements of the white South. Gradually there could have been built up a political party or even parties of the best of the black and white South. The Negroes would have been more than modest in their demands so long as they saw a chance to keep moving toward real freedom. But the master class did not choose this, although some like Wade Hampton of South Carolina, made steps toward it. On the whole, the masters settled definitely upon a purely racial line, recognizing as theirs everything that had a white skin and putting without the pale of sympathy and alliance, everything of Negro descent. By bitter and unyielding social pressure they pounded the whites into a solid phalanx, but in order to do this they had to give up much.

In the first place the leadership of the South passed from the hands of the old slave owners into the hands of the newer town capitalists who were largely merchants and the coming industrial leaders. Some of them represented the older dominant class and some of them the newer poor whites. They were welded, however, into a new economic mastership, less cultivated, more ruthless and more keen in recognizing the possibilities of Negro labor if "controlled" as they proposed to control it. This new leadership, however, did not simply solidify the South, it proceeded to make alliance in the North and to make alliance of the most effective kind, namely economic alliance. The sentimentalism of the war period had in the North changed to the recognition of the grim fact of destroyed capital, dead workers and high prices. The South was a field which could be exploited if peaceful conditions could be reached and the laboring class made sufficiently content and submissive. It was the business then of the "New" South to show to the northern capitalists that by uniting the economic interests of both, they could exploit the Negro laborer and the white laborer—pitting the two classes against each other, keeping out labor unions and building a new industrial South which would pay tremendous returns. This was the program which began with the withdrawal of Northern troops in 1876 and was carried on up to 1890 when it gained political sanction by open laws disfranchising the Negro.

But the experiment was carried on at a terrific cost. First, the Negro could not be cowed and beaten back from his new-found freedom without a mass of force, fraud and actual savagery such as strained the moral fibre of the white South to the utmost. It will be a century before the South recovers from this *débacle* and this explains why this great stretch of land has today so meager an output of science, literature and art and can discuss practically nothing but the "Negro" problem. It explains why the South is the one region in the civilized world where sometimes men are publicly burned alive at the stake.

On the other hand, even this display of force and hatred did not keep the Negro from advancing and the reason for this was that he was in competition with a white laboring class which, despite all efforts and advantages could not outstrip the Negroes and put them wholly under their feet. By judiciously using this rivalry, the Negro gained economic advantage after advantage, and foothold after foothold until today while by no means free and still largely deprived of political rights, we have a mass of 10,000,000 people whose economic condition may be thus described: If we roughly conceive of something like a tenth of the white population as below the line of decent free economic existence, we may guess that a third of the black American population of 12 millions is still in economic serfdom, comparable to condition of the submerged tenth in cities, and held in debt and crime peonage in the sugar, rice and cotton belts. Six other millions are emerging and fighting, in competition with white laborers, a fairly successful battle for rising wages and better conditions. In the last ten years a million of these have been willing and able to move physically from Southern serfdom to the freer air of the North.

The other three millions are as free as the better class of white laborers; and are pushing and carrying the white laborer with them in their grim determination to hold advantages gained and gain others. The Negro's agitation for the right to vote has made any step toward disfranchising the poor white unthinkable, for the white vote is needed to help disfranchise the blacks; the black man is pounding open the doors of exclusive trade guilds; for how can unions exclude whites when Negro competition can break a steel strike? The Negro is making America and the world acknowledge democracy as feasible and desirable for all white folk, for only in this way do they see any possibility of defending their world wide fear of yellow, brown and black folk.

In a peculiar way, then, the Negro in the United States has emancipated democracy, reconstructed the threatened edifice of Freedom and been a sort of eternal test of the sincerity of our democratic ideals. As a Negro minister, J. W. C. Pennington, said in London and Glasgow before the Civil war: "The colored population of the United States has no destiny separate from that of the nation in which they form an integral part. Our destiny is bound up with that of America. Her ship is ours; her pilot is ours; her storms are ours; her calms are ours. If she breaks upon a rock, we break with her. If we, born in America, cannot live upon the same soil upon terms of equality with the descendants of Scotchmen, Englishmen, Irishmen, Frenchmen, Germans, Hungarians, Greeks and Poles, then the fundamental theory of American fails and falls to the ground."

This is still true and it puts the American Negro in a peculiar strategic position with regard to the race problems of the whole world. What do we mean by democracy? Do we mean democracy of the white races and the subjection of the colored races? Or do we mean the gradual working forward to a time when all men will have a voice in government and industry and will be intelligent enough to express the voice?

It is this latter thesis for which the American Negro stands and has stood, and more than any other element in the modern world it has slowly but continuously forced America toward that point and is still forcing. It must be remembered that it was the late Booker T. Washington who planned the beginning of an industrial democracy in the South, based on education, and that in our day the National Association for the Advancement of Colored People, nine-tenths of whose members are Negroes, is the one persistent agency in the United States which is voicing a demand for democracy unlimited by race, sex or religion. American Negroes have even crossed the waters and held three Pan-African Congresses to arouse black men through the world to work for modern democratic development. Thus the emancipation of the Negro slave in America becomes through his own determined effort simply one step toward the emancipation of all men.

VI

The Freedom of Womanhood

How the black woman from her low estate not only united two great human races but helped lift herself and all women to economic independence and self-expression.

The emancipation of woman is, of course, but one phase of the growth of democracy. It deserves perhaps separate treatment because it is an interesting example of the way in which the Negro has helped American democracy.

In the United States in 1920 there were 5,253,695 women of Negro descent; over twelve hundred thousand of these were children, another twelve hundred thousand were girls and young women under twenty, and two and a half million were adults. As a mass these women have but the beginnings of education,—twelve percent of those from sixteen to twenty years of age were unable to write, and twenty-eight percent of those twenty-one years of age and over. These women are passing through, not only a moral, but an economic revolution. Their grandmothers married at twelve and fifteen, but in 1910 twenty-seven percent of these women who had passed fifteen were still single.

Yet these black women toil and toil hard. There were in 1910 two and a half million Negro homes in the United States. Out of these homes walked daily to work two million women and girls over ten years of age,—one half of the colored female population as against a fifth in the case of white women. These, then, are a group of workers, fighting for their daily bread like men; independent and approaching economic freedom! They furnished a million farm laborers, 80,000 farmers, 22,000 teachers, 600,000 servants and washerwomen, and 50,000 in trades and merchandizing. In 1920, 38.9% of colored women were at work as contrasted with 17.2% of native white women. Of the colored women 39% were farming and 50% in service.

The family group, however, which is the ideal of the culture into which these folk have been born, is not based on the idea of an economically independent working mother. Rather its ideal harks back to the sheltered harem with the mother emerging at first as nurse and homemaker, while the man remains the sole breadwinner. Thus the Negro woman more than the women of any other group in America is the protagonist in the fight for an economically independent womanhood in modern countries. Her fight has not been willing or for the most part conscious but it has, nevertheless, been curiously effective in its influence on the working world.

This matter of economic independence is, of course, the central fact in the struggle of women for equality. In the earlier days the slave woman was found to be economically as efficient as the man. Moreover, because of her production of children she became in many ways more valuable; but because she was a field hand the slave family differed from the free family. The children were brought up very largely in common on the plantation, there was comparatively small parental control or real family life and the chief function of the woman was working and not making a home. We can see here pre-figured a type of social development toward which the world is working again for similar and larger reasons. In our modern industrial organization the work of women is being found as valuable as that of men. They are consequently being taken from the home and put into industry and the rapidity by which this process is going on is only kept back by the problem of the child; and more and more the community is taking charge of the education of children for this reason.

In America the work of Negro women has not only pre-figured this development but it has had a direct influence upon it. The Negro woman as laborer, as seamstress, as servant and cook, has come into competition with the white male laborer and with the white woman worker. The fact that she could and did replace the white man as laborer, artisan and servant, showed the possibility of the white woman doing the same thing, and led to it. Moreover, the usual sentimental arguments against women at work were not brought forward in the case of Negro womanhood. Nothing illustrates this so well as the speech of Sojourner Truth before the second National Woman Suffrage Convention, in 1852.

Sojourner Truth came from the lowest of the low, a slave whose children had been sold away from her, a hard, ignorant worker without even a name, who came to this meeting of white women and crouched in a corner against the wall. "Don't let her speak," was repeatedly said to the presiding officer. "Don't get our cause mixed up with abolition and 'niggers'." The discussion became warm, resolutions were presented and argued. Much was said of the superiority of man's intellect, the general helplessness of women and their need for courtesy, the sin of Eve, etc. Most of the white women, being "perfect ladies," according to the ideals of the time, were not used to speaking in public and finally to their dismay the black woman arose from the corner. The audience became silent.

Sojourner Truth was an Amazon nearly six feet high, black, erect and with piercing eyes, and her speech in reply was to the point:

"Dat man ober dar say dat women needs to be helped into carriages, and lifted ober ditches, and to have the best places every whar. Nobody eber help me into carriages, or ober mud puddles, or gives me any best place" (and raising herself to her full height and her voice to a pitch like rolling thunder, she asked), "and ai'n't I a woman? Look at me! Look at my arm!" (And she bared her right arm to the shoulder, showing her tremendous muscular power.) "I have plowed, and planted, and gathered into barns, and no man could head me—and ai'n't I a woman? I could work as much and eat as much as a man (when I could get it), and bear de lash as well—and ai'n't I a woman? I have borne thirteen chilern and seen 'em mos' all sold off into slavery, and when I cried out with a mother's grief, none but Jesus heard—and ai'n't I a woman? Den dey talks 'bout dis ting in de head—what dis dey call it?" ("Intellect," whispered some one near.) "Dat's it honey. What's dat got to do with women's rights or niggers' rights? If my cup won't hold but a pint and yourn holds a quart, wouldn't ye be mean not to let me have my little half-measure full?" . . . She ended by asserting that "If de fust woman God ever made was strong enough to turn the world upside down, all 'lone, dese togedder" (and she glanced her eye over us,) "ought to be able to turn it back and get it right side up again, and now dey is asking to do it, de men better let 'em. . ."

"Amid roars of applause, she turned to her corner, leaving more than one of us with streaming eyes and hearts beating with gratitude. She had taken us up in her strong arms and carried us safely over the slough of difficulty, turning the whole tide in our favor. I have never in my life seen anything like the magical influence that subdued the mobbish spirit of the day and turned the jibes and sneers of an excited crowd into notes of respect and admiration. Hundreds rushed up to shake hands, and congratulate the glorious old mother and bid her God speed on her mission of 'testifying again concerning the wickedness of this 'ere people'."[1]

---

1. Testimony of the presiding officer, Mrs. Frances D. Gage, in *"Narrative of Sojourner Truth,"* 1884, pp. 134–5.

Again and in more concrete ways the Negro woman has influenced America and that is by her personal contact with the family—its men, women and children. As housekeeper, maid and nurse—as confidante, adviser and friend, she was often an integral part of the white family life of the South, and transmitted her dialect, her mannerisms, her quaint philosophy and her boundless sympathy.

Beyond this she became the concubine. It is a subject scarcely to be mentioned today with our conventional morals and with the bitter racial memories swirling about this institution of slavery. Yet the fact remains stark, ugly, painful, beautiful.

Let us regard it dispassionately, remembering that the concubine is as old as the world and that birth is a biological fact. It is usual to speak of the Negro as being the great example of the unassimiliated group in American life. This, of course, is flatly untrue; probably of the strains of blood longest present in America since the discovery by Columbus, the Negro has been less liable to absorption than other groups; but this does not mean that he has not been absorbed and that his blood has not been spread throughout the length and breadth of the land.

"We southern ladies are complimented with the names of wives; but we are only the mistresses of seraglios," said a sister of President Madison; and a Connecticut minister who lived 14 years in Carolina said: "As it relates to amalgamation, I can say, that I have been in respectable families (so-called), where I could distinguish the family resemblance in the slaves who waited upon the table. I once hired a slave who belonged to his own uncle. It is so common for the female slaves to have white children, that little is ever said about it. Very few inquiries are made as to who the father is."[2]

One has only to remember the early histories of cities like Charleston and New Orleans to see what the Negro concubine meant and how she transfigured America. Paul Alliot said in his reflections of Louisiana in 1803: "The population of that city counting the people of all colors is only twelve thousand souls. Mulattoes and Negroes are openly protected by the Government. He who strikes one of those persons, even though he had run away from him, would be severely punished. Also twenty whites could be counted in the prisons of New Orleans against one man of color. The wives and daughters of the latter are much sought after by the white men, and white women at times esteem well-built men of

---

2. Goodell, *Slave Code*, p. 111.

W.E.B. DU BOIS

color."[3] The same writer tells us that few white men marry, preferring to live with their slaves or with women of color.

A generation later the situation was much the same in spite of reaction. In 1818, a traveler says of New Orleans: "Here may be seen in the same crowds, Quadroons, Mulattoes, Samboes, Mustizos, Indians and Negroes; and there are other commixtures which are not yet classified."[4]

"The minor distinctions of complexion and race so fiercely adhered to by the Creoles of the old regime were at their height at this time. The glory and shame of the city were her quadroons and octoroons, apparently constituting two aristocratic circles of society, the one as elegant as the other, the complexions the same, the men the same, the women different in race, but not in color, nor in dress nor in jewels. Writers on fire with the romance of this continental city love to speak of the splendors of the French Opera House, the first place in the country where grand opera was heard, and tell of the tiers of beautiful women with their jewels and airs and graces. Above the orchestra circle were four tiers; the first filled with the beautiful dames of the city; the second filled with a second array of beautiful women, attired like those of the first, with no apparent difference; yet these were the octoroons and quadroons, whose beauty and wealth were all the passports needed. The third was for the *hoi polloi* of the white race, and the fourth for the people of color whose color was more evident. It was a veritable sandwich of races."[5]

Whatever judgment we may pass upon all this and however we may like or dislike it, the fact remains that the colored slave women became the medium through which two great races were united in America. Moreover it is the fashion to assume that all this was merely infiltration of white blood into the black; but we must remember it was just as surely infiltration of black blood into white America and not even an extraordinary drawing of the color line against all visible Negro blood has ever been able to trace its true limits.

There is scarcely an American, certainly none of the South and no Negro American, who does not know in his personal experience of Americans of Negro descent who either do not know or do not

3. Robertson, *Louisiana under the Rule of Spain,* Vol. I, pp. 67, 103, 111; Dunbar-Nelson, in *Journal of Negro History,* Vol. 2, p. 56.
4. Dunbar-Nelson, *loc. cit.*
5. Dunbar-Nelson, *op. cit.,* p. 62; Martineau, *Society in America,* p. 326ff.

acknowledge their African ancestry. This is their right, if they do know, and a matter of but passing importance if they do not. But without doubt the spiritual legacy of Africa has been spread through this mingling of blood. First, of course, we may think of those more celebrated cases where the mixed blood is fairly well known but nevertheless the man has worked and passed as a white man. One of the earliest examples was that of Alexander Hamilton. Alexander Hamilton was a case in point of the much disputed "Creole" blood. Theoretically the Creole was a person of European descent on both sides born in the West Indies or America; but as there were naturally few such persons in earlier times because of the small number of European women who came to America, those descendants of European fathers and mulatto mothers were in practice called "Creole" and consequently it soon began to be *prima facie* evidence, in the West Indies, that an illegitimate child of a white father was of Negro descent. Alexander Hamilton was such an illegitimate child. He had colored relatives whose descendants still live in America and he was currently reported to be colored in the island of Nevis. Further than this, of course, proof is impossible. But to those who have given careful attention to the subject, little further proof is needed.

To this can be added a long list of American notables,—bishops, generals and members of Congress. Many writers and artists have found hidden inspiration in their Negro blood and from the first importation in the fifteenth century down to today there has been a continual mingling of white and Negro blood in the United States both within and without the bonds of wedlock that neither law nor slavery nor cruel insult and contempt has been able to stop.

Besides these influences in economics and the home there has come the work of Negro women in revolt which cannot be forgotten. We mention two cases.

Harriet Tubman was a woman absolutely illiterate, who, from 1849 down to the Civil War, spent her time journeying backward and forward between the free and slave states and leading hundreds of black fugitives into freedom. Thousands of dollars were put upon her head as rewards for her capture; and she was continually sought by northern abolitionists and was a confidant of John Brown. During the War, she acted as a spy, guide and nurse and in all these days, worked without pay or reward. William H. Seward said: "A nobler, higher spirit or truer, seldom dwells in the human form," and Wendell Phillips added: "In my opinion there are few captains, perhaps few colonels who have done more for the loyal cause since the War began and few men who did before that time more for the colored race than our fearless and most sagacious friend, Harriet." Abraham Lincoln gave her ready audience.[6]

Quite a different kind of woman and yet strangely effective and influential was Mammy Pleasants of California. Here was a colored woman who became one of the shrewdest business minds of the State. She anticipated the development in oil; she was the trusted confidant of many of the California pioneers like Ralston, Mills and Booth and for years was a power in San Francisco affairs. Yet, she held her memories, her hatreds, her deep designs and throughout a life that was perhaps more than unconventional, she treasured a bitter hatred for slavery and a certain contempt for white people.

As a field hand in Georgia she had attracted the attention of a planter by her intelligence and was bought and sent to Boston for training. Here she was made a household drudge and eventually married Alexander Smith who was associated with Garrison and the abolitionists. With $50,000 from his estate, she came to California and made a fortune. The epitaph which she wanted on her tombstone was, "She was a friend of John Brown." When she first heard of the projects of Brown she determined to help him and April 5, 1858, when John Brown was captured at Harper's Ferry, they found upon him a letter reading: "The ax is laid at the foot of the tree; when the first blow is struck there will be more money to help." This was signed by three initials which the authorities thought were "W. E. P."—in fact they were "M. E. P." and stood for Mammy Pleasants. She had come East the spring before with a $30,000 United States draft which she changed into coin and meeting John Brown in Chatham or Windsor, Canada, had turned this money over to him. It was agreed, however, that he was not to strike his blow until she had helped to arouse the slaves. Disguised as a jockey, she went South and while there heard of Brown's raid and capture at Harper's ferry. She fled to New York and finally reached California on a ship that came around Cape Horn, sailing in the steerage under an assumed name.

Mammy Pleasants "always wore a poke bonnet and a plaid shawl," and she was "very black with thin lips" and "she handled more money during pioneers days in California than any other colored person."[7]

---

6. Brownie's Book, March, 1921.

7. Beasley, *Negro Trail Blazers*, pp. 95–7.

Here then, we have the types of colored women who rose out of the black mass of slaves not only to guide their own folk but to influence the nation.

We have noted then the Negro woman in America as a worker tending to emancipate all women workers; as a mother nursing the white race and uniting the black and white race; as a conspirator urging forward emancipation in various sorts of ways; and we have finally only to remember that today the women of America who are doing humble but on the whole the most effective work in the social uplift of the lowly, not so much by money as by personal contact, are the colored women. Little is said or known about it but in thousands of churches and social clubs, in missionary societies and fraternal organizations, in unions like the National Association of Colored Women, these workers are founding and sustaining orphanages and old folk homes; distributing personal charity and relief; visiting prisoners; helping hospitals; teaching children; and ministering to all sorts of needs. Their work, as it comes now and then in special cases to the attention of individuals of the white world, forms a splendid bond of encouragement and sympathy, and helps more than most realize in minimizing racial difficulties and encouraging human sympathy.[8]

8. Cf. Annual Reports National Association of Colored Women; Atlanta University Publications, No. 14.

VII

The American Folk Song

*How black folk sang their sorrow songs in the land of their bondage
and made this music the only American folk music.*

L ittle of beauty has America given the world save the rude grandeur
God himself stamped on her bosom; the human spirit in this new
world has expressed itself in vigor and ingenuity rather than in beauty.
And so by fateful chance the Negro folk-song—the rhythmic cry of
the slave—stands today not simply as the sole American music, but
as the most beautiful expression of human experience born this side
the seas. It has been neglected, it has been persistently mistaken and
misunderstood; but notwithstanding, it still remains as the singular
spiritual heritage of the nation and the greatest gift of the Negro
people."[1]

Around the Negro folk-song there has arisen much of controversy
and of misunderstanding. For a long time they were utterly neglected;
then every once in a while and here and there they forced themselves
upon popular attention. In the thirties, they emerged and in tunes like
"Near the lake where droop the willow" and passed into current song
or were caricatured by the minstrels. Then came Stephen Foster who
accompanied a mulatto maid often to the Negro church and heard
the black folk sing; he struck a new note in songs like "Old Kentucky
Home," "Old Folks at Home" and "Nellie was a Lady." But it was left
to war and emancipation to discover the real primitive beauty of this
music to the world.

When northern men and women who knew music, met the slaves at
Port Royal after its capture by Federal troops, they set down these songs
in their original form for the first time so that the world might hear
and sing them. The sea islands of the Carolinas where these meetings
took place "with no third witness" were filled with primitive black folk,
uncouth in appearance, and queer in language, but their singing was
marvellous. Thomas Wentworth Higginson and Miss McKim and

---

1. Du Bois, *Souls of Black Folk,* Chapter No. 14.

others collected these songs in 1867, making the first serious study of Negro American music. The preface said:

"The musical capacity of the Negro race has been recognized for so many years that it is hard to explain why no systematic effort has hitherto been made to collect and preserve their melodies. More than thirty years ago those plantation songs made their appearance which were so extraordinarily popular for a while; and if 'Coal-black Rose,' 'Zip Coon' and 'Ole Virginny nebber tire' have been succeeded by spurious imitations, manufactured to suit the somewhat sentimental taste of our community, the fact that these were called 'Negro melodies' was itself a tribute to the musical genius of the race.

"The public had well-nigh forgotten these genuine slave songs, and with them the creative power from which they sprung, when a fresh interest was excited through the educational mission to the Port Royal Islands in 1861."[2]

Still the world listened only half credulously until the Fisk Jubilee Singers sang the slave songs "so deeply into the world's heart that it can never wholly forget them again." The story of the Fisk Jubilee singers is romantic. In abandoned barracks at Nashville hundreds of colored children were being taught and the dream of a Negro University had risen in the minds of the white teachers. But even the lavish contribution for missionary work, which followed the war, had by 1870 begun to fall off. It happened that the treasurer of Fisk, George L. White, loved music. He began to instruct the Fisk students in singing and he used the folk-songs. He met all sorts of difficulties. The white people of the nation and especially the conventional church folk who were sending missionary money, were not interested in "minstrel ditties." The colored people looked upon these songs as hateful relics of slavery. Nevertheless, Mr. White persisted, gathered a pioneer band of singers and in 1871 started north.

"It was the sixth day of October in the year of our Lord, one thousand eight hundred and seventy-one, when George L. White started out from Fisk School with his eleven students to raise money, that Fisk might live. Professor Adam K. Spence, who was principal of the school, gave Mr. White all the money in his possession save one dollar, which he held back, that the treasury might not be empty. While friends and parents wept, waved, and feared, the train puffed out of the station. All

---

2. W. F. Allen and others, *Slave Songs of the United States,* New York, 1867.

sorts of difficulties, obstacles, oppositions and failures faced them until through wonderful persistence, they arrived at Oberlin, Ohio. Here the National Council of Congregational Churches was in session. After repeated efforts, Mr. White gained permission for his singers to render one song. Many of the members of the Council objected vigorously to having such singers. During the time of the session the weather had been dark and cloudy. The sun had not shone one moment, it had not cast one ray upon the village. The singers went into the gallery of the church, unobserved by all save the moderator and a few who were on the rostrum. At a lull in the proceeding, there floated sweetly to the ears of the audience the measures of 'Steal Away to Jesus.' Suddenly the sun broke through the clouds, shone through the windows upon the singers, and verily they were a heavenly choir. For a time the Council forgot its business and called for more and more. It was at this point that Henry Ward Beecher almost demanded of Mr. White that he cancel all engagements and come straight to his church in Brooklyn. . ."

The New York papers ridiculed and sneered at Beecher's "nigger minstrels." But Beecher stuck to his plan and it was only a matter of hearing them once when audiences went into ecstasies.

"When the Metropolitan newspapers called the company 'Nigger Minstrels,' Mr. White was face to face with a situation as serious as it was awkward. His company had no appropriate name, and the odium of the title attributed by the New York newspapers pained him intensely. If they were to be known as 'Nigger Minstrels,' they could never realize his vision; they were both handicapped and checkmated, and their career was dead. . . The suggestiveness of the Hebrew Jubilee had been borne in upon his mind and with joy of a deep conviction he exclaimed, 'Children, you are the Jubilee Singers'."[3]

For seven years the career of this company of Jubilee Singers was a continual triumph. They crowded the concert halls of New England; they began to send money back to Fisk; they went to Great Britain and sang before Queen Victoria, Lord Shaftesbury and Mr. Gladstone. Gladstone cried: "It's wonderful!" Queen Victoria wept. Moody, the evangelist, brought them again and again to his London meetings, and the singers were loaded with gifts. Then they went to Germany, and again Kings and peasants listened to them. In seven years they were able to pay not only all of their own expenses but to send $150,000 in

---

3. G. D. Pike, *The Jubilee Singers*, New York, 1873.

cash to Fisk University, and out of this money was built Jubilee Hall, on the spot that was once a slave market. "There it stands, lifting up its grateful head to God in His heaven."

For a long time after some people continued to sneer at Negro music. They declared it was a "mere imitation," that it had little intrinsic value, that it was not the music of Negroes at all. Gradually, however, this attitude has completely passed and today critics vie with each other in giving tribute to this wonderful gift of the black man to America.

Damrosch says: "The Negro's music isn't ours, it is the Negro's. It has become a popular form of musical expression and is interesting, but it is not ours. Nothing more characteristic of a race exists, but it is characteristic of the Negro, not the American race. Through it a primitive people poured out its emotions with wonderful expressiveness. It no more expresses our emotions than the Indian music does."

Recently, numbers of serious studies of the Negro folk-song have been made. James Weldon Johnson says: "In the 'spirituals,' or slave songs, the Negro has given America not only its only folk-songs, but a mass of noble music. I never think of this music but that I am struck by the wonder, the miracle of its production. How did the men who originated these songs manage to do it? The sentiments are easily accounted for; they are, for the most part, taken from the Bible. But the melodies, where did they come from? Some of them so weirdly sweet, and others so wonderfully strong. Take, for instance, 'Go Down, Moses'; I doubt that there is a stronger theme in the whole musical literature of the world.

"It is to be noted that whereas the chief characteristic of Ragtime is rhythm, the chief characteristic of the 'spirituals' is melody. The melodies of 'Steal Away to Jesus,' 'Swing Low, Sweet Chariot,' 'Nobody Knows de Trouble I See,' 'I couldn't hear Nobody Pray,' 'Deep River,' 'O, Freedom Over Me,' and many others of these songs possess a beauty that is—what shall I say? Poignant. In the riotous rhythms of Ragtime the Negro expressed his irrepressible buoyancy, his keen response to the sheer joy of living; in the 'spirituals' he voiced his sense of beauty and his deep religious feeling."[4]

H. E. Krehbiel says: "There was sunshine as well as gloom in the life of the black slaves in the Southern colonies and States, and so we have songs which are gay as well as grave; but as a rule the finest songs are

4. James Weldon Johnson, *Book of American Negro Poetry*, New York, 1922.

the fruits of suffering undergone and the hope of the deliverance from bondage which was to come with translation to heaven after death. The oldest of them are the most beautiful, and many of the most striking have never yet been collected, partly because they contained elements, melodic as well as rhythmical, which baffled the ingenuity of the early collectors. Unfortunately, trained musicians have never entered upon the field, and it is to be feared that it is now too late. The peculiarities which the collaborators on 'Slave Songs of the United States' recognized, but could not imprison on the written page, were elements which would have been of especial interest to the student of art.

"Is it not the merest quibble to say that these songs are not American? They were created in America under American influences and by people who are Americans in the same sense that any other element of our population is American—every element except the aboriginal. . . Is it only an African who can sojourn here without becoming an American and producing American things; is it a matter of length of stay in the country? Scarcely that; or some Negroes would have at least as good a claim on the title as the descendants of the Puritans and Pilgrims. Negroes figure in the accounts of his voyages to America made by Columbus. . . A year before the English colonists landed on Plymouth Rock Negroes were sold into servitude in Virginia."[5]

The most gifted and sympathetic student of the folk-song in Africa and America was Natalie Curtis, and it is scarcely necessary to add to what she has so carefully and sympathetically written. She has traced the connection between African and Afro-American music which has always been assumed but never carefully proven. The African rhythm, through the use of the drum as a leading instrument, produced musical emphasis which we call syncopation. Primitive music usually shows rhythm and melody of the voice sung in unison. But in Africa, part singing was developed long before it appeared in Europe. The great difference between the music of Africa and the music of Europe lies in rhythm; in Europe the music is accented on the regular beats of the music while in Africa the accents fall often on the unstressed beats. It is this that coming down through the Negro folk-song in America has produced what is known as ragtime.

---

5. H. E. Krehbiel, *Afro-American Folksongs,* New York, 1914; cf. also John W. Work, *Folksong of the American Negro,* Nashville, Tenn., 1915.

Mrs. Curtis Burlin shows that the folk-song of the African in America can be traced direct to Africa: "As a creator of beauty the black man is capable of contributing to the great art of the world.

"The Negro's pronounced gift for music is today widely recognized. That gift, brought to America in slave-ships, was nurtured by that mother of woe, human slavery, till out of suffering and toil there sprang a music which speaks to the heart of mankind—the prayer-song of the American Negro. In Africa is rooted the parent stem of that out-flowering of Negro folk-song in other lands.

"Through the Negro this country is vocal with a folk-music intimate, complete and beautiful. It is the Negro music with its by-product of 'ragtime' that today most widely influences the popular song-life of America, and Negro rhythms have indeed captivated the world at large. Nor may we foretell the impress that the voice of the slave will leave upon the art of the country—a poetic justice, this! For the Negro everywhere discriminated against, segregated and shunned, mobbed and murdered—he it is whose melodies are on all our lips, and whose rhythms impel our marching feet in a 'war for democracy.' The irresistible music that wells up from this sunny and unresentful people is hummed and whistled, danced to and marched to, laughed over and wept over, by high and low and rich and poor throughout the land. The downtrodden black man whose patient religious faith has kept his heart still unembittered, is fast becoming the singing voice of all America. And in his song we hear a prophecy of the dignity and worth of Negro genius."[6]

The Negro folk-song entered the Church and became the prayer song and the sorrow song, still with its haunting melody but surrounded by the inhibitions of a cheap theology and a conventional morality. But the musical soul of a race unleashed itself violently from these bonds and in the saloons and brothels of the Mississippi bottoms and gulf coast flared to that crimson license of expression known as "ragtime," "jazz" and the more singular "blues" retaining with all their impossible words the glamour of rhythm and wild joy. White composers hastily followed with songs like "A Hot Time in the Old Town Tonight," and numerous successors in popular favor.

---

6. Natalie Curtis-Burlin, *Negro Folksongs,* 4 books, 1918–19; *Songs and Tales from the Dark Continent,* 1920.

Out of ragtime grew a further development through both white and black composers. The "blues," a curious and intriguing variety of love song from the levees of the Mississippi, became popular and was spread by the first colored man who was able to set it down, W. C. Handy of Memphis. Other men, white and colored, from Stephen Foster to our day, have taken another side of Negro music and developed its haunting themes and rippling melody into popular songs and into high and fine forms of modern music, until today the influence of the Negro reaches every part of American music, of many foreign masters like Dvorak; and certainly no program of concert music could be given in America without voicing Negro composers and Negro themes.

We can best end this chapter with the word of a colored man: "But there is something deeper than the sensuousness of beauty that makes for the possibilities of the Negro in the realm of the arts, and that is the soul of the race. The wail of the old melodies and the plaintive quality that is ever present in the Negro voice are but the reflection of a background of tragedy. No race can rise to the greatest heights of art until it has yearned and suffered. The Russians are a case in point. Such has been their background in oppression and striving that their literature and art are today marked by an unmistakable note of power. The same future beckons to the American Negro. There is something very elemental about the heart of the race, something that finds its origin in the African forest, in the sighing of the night wind, and in the falling of the stars. There is something grim and stern about it all, too, something that speaks of the lash, of the child torn from its mother's bosom, of the dead body riddled with bullets and swinging all night from a limb by the roadside."[7]

---

7. Benjamin Brawley, *Negro in Literature and Art.*

VIII

NEGRO ART AND LITERATURE

How the tragic story of the black slave has become a central theme of the story of America and has inspired literature and created art.

The Negro is primarily an artist. The usual way of putting this is to speak disdainfully of his "sensuous" nature. This means that the only race which has held at bay the life destroying forces of the tropics, has gained therefrom in some slight compensation a sense of beauty, particularly for sound and color, which characterizes the race. The Negro blood which flowed in the veins of many of the mightiest of the Pharaohs accounts for much of Egyptian art, and indeed Egyptian civilization owes much in its origin to the development of the large strain of Negro blood which manifested itself in every grade of Egyptian society.

Semitic civilization also had its Negroid influences, and these continually turn toward art as in the case of black Nosseyeb, one of the five great poets of Damascus under the Ommiades, and the black Arabian hero, Antar. It was therefore not to be wondered at that in modern days one of the greatest of modern literatures, the Russian, should have been founded by Pushkin, the grandson of a full blooded Negro, and that among the painters of Spain was the mulatto slave, Gomez. Back of all this development by way of contact, come the artistic sense of the indigenous Negro as shown in the stone figures of Sherbro, the bronzes of Benin, the marvelous hand work in iron and other metals which has characterized the Negro race so long that archaeologists today, with less and less hesitation, are ascribing the discovery of the welding of iron to the Negro race.

Beyond the specific ways in which the Negro has contributed to American art stands undoubtedly his spirit of gayety and the exotic charm which his presence has loaned the parts of America which were spiritually free enough to enjoy it. In New Orleans, for instance, after the war of 1812 and among the free people of color there was a beautiful blossoming of artistic life which the sordid background of slavery had to work hard to kill. The "people of color" grew in number and waxed wealthy. Famous streets even today bear testimony of their old importance. Congo Square in the old Creole quarter where Negroes danced the weird "Bamboula" long before colored Coleridge-Taylor made it immortal and Gottschalk wrote his Negro dance. Camp street and Julia street took their names from the old Negro field and from the woman who owned land along the Canal. Americans and Spanish both tried to get the support and sympathy of the free Negroes. The followers of Aaron Burr courted them.

"Writers describing the New Orleans of this period agree in presenting a picture of a continental city, most picturesque, most un-American, and as varied in color as a street of Cairo. There they saw French, Spaniards, English, Bohemians, Negroes, mulattoes, varied clothes, picturesque white dresses of the fairer women, brilliant cottons of the darker ones. The streets, banquettes, we should say, were bright with color, the nights filled with song and laughter. Through the scene, the people of color add the spice of color; in the life, they add the zest of romance."[1]

Music is always back of this gay Negro spirit and the folk song which the Negro brought to America was developed not simply by white men but by the Negro himself. Musicians and artists sprung from the Louisiana group. There was Eugene Warburg who distinguished himself as a sculptor in Italy. There was Victor Sejour who became a poet and composer in France, Dubuclet became a musician in Bordeaux and the seven Lamberts taught and composed in America, France and Brazil. One of the brothers Sydney was decorated for his work by the King of Portugal. Edmund Dèdè became a director of a leading orchestra in France.[2]

Among other early colored composers of music are J. Hemmenway who lived in Philadelphia in the twenties; A. J. Conner of Philadelphia between 1846–57 published numbers of compositions; in the seventies Justin Holland was well known as a composer in Cleveland, Ohio; Samuel Milady, known by his stage name as Sam Lucas, was born in 1846 and died in 1916. He wrote many popular ballads, among them "Grandfather's Clock Was Too Tall For The Shelf." George Melbourne, a Negro street minstrel, composed "Listen to the Mocking-Bird," although a white man got the credit. James Bland wrote "Carry me Back to Ole Virginny"; Gussie L. Davis composed popular music at Cincinnati.[3]

---

1. Alice Dunbar-Nelson in *Journal of Negro History,* Vol. 2, p. 55.
2. Washington, *Story of the Negro,* Vol. 2, pp. 276–7.
3. Cf. Benjamin Brawley, *The Negro in Literature and Art,* New York, 1921.

Coming to our day we remember that the Anglo-African Samuel Coleridge-Taylor received much of his inspiration from his visits to the American Negro group; then comes Harry T. Burleigh, perhaps the greatest living song writer in America. Among his works are "Five Songs" by Laurence Hope; "The Young Warrior," which became one of the greatest of the war songs; "The Grey Wolf" and "Ethiopia Saluting the Colors." His adaptations of Negro folk-songs are widely known and he assisted Dvorak in his "New World Symphony." R. Nathaniel Dett has written "Listen to the Lambs," a carol widely known, and "The Magnolia Suite." Rosamond Johnson wrote "Under the Bamboo Tree" and a dozen popular favorites beside choruses and marches. Clarence Cameron White has composed and adapted and Maud Cuney Hare has revived and explained Creole music. Edmund T. Jenkins has won medals at the Royal Academy in London. Among the colored performers on the piano are R. Augustus Lawson, who has often been soloist at the concerts of the Hartford Philharmonic Orchestra; Hazel Harrison, a pupil of Busoni; and Helen Hagen who took the Sanford scholarship at Yale. Carl Diton is a pianist who has transcribed many Negro melodies. Melville Charlton has done excellent work on the organ.

Then we must remember the Negro singers, the "Black Swan" of the early 19th century whose voice compared with Jenny Lind's; the Hyer sisters, Flora Batson, Florence Cole Talbert, and Roland W. Hayes, the tenor whose fine voice has charmed London, Paris and Vienna and who is now one of the leading soloists of the Boston Symphony Orchestra.

The Negro has been one of the greatest originators of dancing in the United States and in the world. He created the "cake walk" and most of the steps in the "clog" dance which has so enthralled theatre audiences. The modern dances which have swept over the world like the "Tango" and "Turkey Trot" originated among the Negroes of the West Indies. The Vernon Castles always told their audiences that their dances were of Negro origin.[4]

We turn now to other forms of art and more particularly literature. Here the subjects naturally divides itself into three parts: *first*, the influence which the Negro has had on American literature,—and *secondly*, the development of a literature for and by Negroes. And lastly

---

4. Cf. Preface to James Weldon Johnson's *The Book of American Negro Poetry*, New York, 1922.

the number of Negroes who have gained a place in National American literature.

From the earliest times the presence of the black man in America has inspired American writers. Among the early Colonial writers the Negro was a subject as, for instance, in Samuel Sewall's "Selling of Joseph," the first American anti-slavery tract published in 1700. But we especially see in the influence of the Negro's condition in the work of the masters of the 19th century, like Ralph Waldo Emerson, John Greenleaf Whittier, James Russell Lowell, Walt Whitman, Julia Ward Howe, Harriet Beecher Stowe and Lydia Maria Child. With these must be named the orators Wendell Phillips, Charles Sumner, John C. Calhoun, Henry Ward Beecher. In our own day, we have had the writers of fiction, George U. Cable, Thomas Nelson Page, Thomas Dixon, Ruth McEnery Stewart, William Dean Howells, Thomas Wentworth Higginson.

It may be said that the influence of the Negro here is a passive influence and yet one must remember that it would be inconceivable to have an American literature, even that written by white men, and not have the Negro as a subject. He has been the lay figure, but after all, the figure has been alive, it has moved, it has talked, felt and influenced.

In the minds of these and other writers how has the Negro been portrayed? It is a fascinating subject which I can but barely touch: in the days of Shakespeare and Southerne the black man of fiction was a man, a brave, fine, if withal over-trustful and impulsive, hero. In science he was different but equal, cunning in unusual but mighty possibilities. Then with the slave trade he suddenly became a clown and dropped from sight. He emerged slowly beginning about 1830 as a dull stupid but contented slave, capable of doglike devotion, superstitious and incapable of education. Then, in the abolition controversy he became a victim, a man of sorrows, a fugitive chased by bloodhounds, a beautiful raped octoroon, a crucified Uncle Tom, but a lay figure, objectively pitiable but seldom subjectively conceived. Suddenly a change came after Reconstruction. The black man was either a faithful old "Befoh de wah" darky worshipping lordly white folk, or a frolicking ape, or a villain, a sullen scoundrel, a violator of womanhood, a low thief and misbirthed monster. He was sub-normal and congenitally incapable. He was represented as an unfit survival of Darwinian natural selection. Philanthropy and religion stood powerless before his pigmy brain and undeveloped morals. In a "thousands years"? Perhaps. But at present, an upper beast. Out of this today he is slowly but tentatively, almost apologetically rising—a somewhat deserving, often poignant, but hopeless figure; a man whose only proper end is dramatic suicide physically or morally. His trouble is natural and inborn inferiority, slight by scientific measurement but sufficient to make absolute limits to his possibilities, save in exceptional cases.

And here we stand today. As a normal human being reacting humanly to human problems the Negro has never appeared in the fiction or the science of white writers, with a bare half dozen exceptions; while to the white southerner who "knows him best" he is always an idiot or a monster, and he sees him as such, no matter what is before his very eyes. And yet, with all this, the Negro has held the stage. In the South he is everything. You cannot discuss religion, morals, politics, social life, science, earth or sky, God or devil without touching the Negro. It is a perennial and continuous and continual subject of books, editorials, sermons, lectures and smoking car confabs. In the north and west while seldom in the center, the Negro is always in the wings waiting to appear or screaming shrill lines off stage. What would intellectual America do if she woke some fine morning to find no "Negro" Problem?

Coming now to the slowly swelling stream of a distinct group literature, by and primarily for the Negro, we enter a realm only partially known to white Americans. First, there come the rich mass of Negro folk lore transplanted from Africa and developed in America. A white writer, Joel Chandler Harris, first popularized "Uncle Remus" and "Brer Rabbit" for white America; but he was simply the deft and singularly successful translator—the material was Negroid and appears repeatedly among the black peasants and various forms and versions. Take for instance the versions of the celebrated tar-baby story of Joel Chandler Harris. C. C. Jones took down a striking version apparently direct from Negro lips early in the 19th century:

"'Do Buh Wolf, bun me: broke me neck, but don't trow me in de brier patch. Lemme dead one time. Don't tarrify me no mo.' Buh Wolf yet bin know wuh Buh Rabbit up teh. Eh tink eh bin guine tare Bur Rabbit hide off. So, wuh eh do? Eh loose Buh Rabbit from de spakleberry bush, an eh tek um by de hine leg, an eh swing um roun', en eh trow um way in de tick brier patch fuh tare eh hide and cratch eh yeye out. De minnit Buh Rabbit drap in de brier patch, eh cock up eh tail, eh jump, an holler back to Buh Wolf: 'Good bye, Budder! Dis de place me mammy fotch me up,—dis de place me mammy fotch me up.' An eh gone before Buh Wolf kin ketch um. Buh Rabbit too scheemy."

W.E.B. DU BOIS

The Harris version shows the literary touch added by the white man. But the Negro version told by Jones has all the meat of the primitive tale.

Next we note the folk rhymes and poetry of Negroes, sometimes accompanying their music and sometimes not. A white instructor in English literature at the University of Virgina says:

"Of all the builders of the nation the Negro alone has created a species of lyric verse that all the world may recognize as a distinctly American production."

T. W. Talley, a Negro, has recently published an exhaustive collection of these rhymes. They form an interesting collection of poetry often crude and commonplace but with here and there touches of real poetry and quaint humor.[5]

The literary expression of Negroes themselves has had continuous development in America since the eighteenth century.[6] It may however be looked upon from two different points of view: We may think of the writing of Negroes as self-expression and as principally for themselves. Here we have a continuous line of writers. Only a few of these, however would we think of as contributing to American literature as such and yet this inner, smaller stream of Negro literature overflows faintly at first and now evidently more and more into the wider stream of American literature; on the other hand there have been figures in American literature who happen to be of Negro descent and who are but vaguely to be identified with the group stream as such. Both these points of view are interesting but let us first take up the succession of authors who form a group literature by and for Negroes.

As early as the eighteenth century, and even before the Revolutionary War the first voices of Negro authors were heard in the United States. Phyllis Wheatley, the black poetess, was easily the pioneer, her first poems appearing in 1773, and other editions in 1774 and 1793. Her earliest poem was in memory of George Whitefield. She was honored by Washington and leading Englishmen and was as a writer above the level of her American white contemporaries.

She was followed by Richard Allen, first Bishop of the African Methodist Church whose autobiography, published in 1793 was the

---

5. T. W. Talley, *Negro Folk Rhymes*.

6. Cf. W. E. B. Du Bois, *The Negro in Literature and Art* (Annals American Academy, Sept., 1913).

beginning of that long series of personal appears and narratives of which Booker T. Washington's "Up From Slavery" was the latest. Benjamin Banneker's almanacs represented the first scientific work of American Negroes, and began to be issued in 1792.

Coming now to the first decades of the nineteenth century we find some essays on freedom by the African Society of Boston, and an apology for the new Negro church formed in Philadelphia. Paul Cuffe, disgusted with America, wrote an early account of Sierra Leone, while the celebrated Lemuel Haynes, ignoring the race question, dipped deeply into the New England theological controversy about 1815. In 1829 came the first full-voiced, almost hysterical, protest against slavery and the color line in David Walker's Appeal which aroused Southern legislatures to action. This was followed by the earliest Negro conventions which issued interesting minutes; two appeals against disfranchisement in Pennsylvania appeared in this decade, one written by Robert Purvis, who also wrote a biography of his father-in-law, Mr. James Forten, and the other appeal written by John Bowers and others. The life of Gustavus Vassa, also known by his African name of Olaudah Equiana, was published in America in 1837 continuing the interesting personal narratives.

In 1840 some strong writers began to appear. Henry Highland Garnet and J. W. C. Pennington preached powerful sermons and gave some attention to Negro history in their pamphlets: R. B. Lewis made a more elaborate attempt at Negro history. Whitfield's poems appeared in 1846, and William Wells Brown began a career of writing which lasted from 1847 until after the Civil War. He began his literary career by the publication of his "Narrative of a Fugitive Slave" in 1847. This was followed by a novel in 1853, "Sketches" from abroad in 1855, a play in 1858, "The Black Man" in 1863, "The Negro in the American Rebellion" in 1867, and "The Rising Son" in 1874. The Colored Convention in Cincinnati and Cleveland published reports in this decade and Bishop Loguen wrote his life history. In 1845 Douglass' autobiography made its first appearance, destined to run through endless editions until the last in 1893. Moreover it was in 1841 that the first Negro magazine appeared in America, edited by George Hogarth and published by the A. M. E. Church.

In the fifties James Whitfield published further poems, and a new poet arose in the person of Frances E. W. Harper, a woman of no little ability who died lately; Martin R. Delaney and William Cooper Nell wrote further of Negro history, Nell especially making valuable contributions of the history of the Negro soldiers. Three interesting biographies were added in this decade to the growing number; Josiah Henson, Samuel C. Ward and Samuel Northrop; while Catto, leaving general history came down to the better known history of the Negro church.

In the sixties slave narratives multiplied, like that of Linda Brent, while two studies of Africa based on actual visits were made by Robert Campbell and Dr. Alexander Crummell; William Douglass and Bishop Daniel Payne continued the history of the Negro church, and William Wells Brown carried forward his work in general Negro history. In this decade, too, Bishop Tanner began his work in Negro theology.

Most of the Negro talent in the seventies was taken up in politics; the older men like Bishop Wayman wrote of their experiences; Sojourner Truth added her story to the slave narratives. A new poet arose in the person of A. A. Whitman, while James Monroe Trotter was the first to take literary note of the musical ability of his race. Robert Brown Elliott stirred the nation by his eloquence in Congress. The Fisk edition of the Songs of the Jubilee Singers appeared.

In the eighties there are signs of unrest and conflicting streams of thought. On the one hand the rapid growth of the Negro church is shown by the writers on church subjects like Moore and Wayman. The historical spirit was especially strong. Still wrote of the Underground Railroad; Simmons issued his interesting biographical dictionary, and the greatest historian of the race appeared when George W. Williams issued his two-volume history of the Negro Race in America. The political turmoil was reflected in Langston's Freedom and Citizenship, Fortune's Black and White, and Straker's New South, and found its bitterest arraignment in Turner's pamphlets; but with all this went other new thought: Scarborough published "First Greek Lessons"; Bishop Payne issued his Treatise on Domestic Education, and Stewart studied Liberia.

In the nineties came histories, essays, novels and poems, together with biographies and social studies. The history was represented by Payne's History of the A. M. E. Church, Hood's "One Hundred Years of the A. M. E. Zion Church, Anderson's sketch of Negro Presbyterianism and Hagood's Colored Man in the M. E. Church; general history of the older type was represented by R. L. Perry's Cushite and of the newer type in E. A. Johnson's histories, while one of the secret societies found their historian in Brooks; Crogman's essays appeared and Archibald Grimke's biographies. The race question was discussed in Frank Grimke's published sermons, social studies were made by Penn, Wright, Mossell, Crummell, Majors and others. Most notable, however, was the rise of the Negro novelist and poet with national recognition: Frances Harper was still writing and Griggs began his racial novels, but both of these spoke primarily to the Negro race; on the other hand, Chesnutt's six novels and Dunbar's inimitable works spoke of the whole nation. J. T. Wilson's "Black Phalanx," the most complete study of the Negro soldier, came in these years.

Booker T. Washington's work began with his address at Atlanta in 1895, "Up From Slavery" in 1901, "Working with the Hands" in 1904, and "The Man Farthest Down" in 1912. The American Negro Academy, a small group, began the publication of occasional papers in 1897 and has published a dozen or more numbers including a "Symposium on the Negro and the Elective Franchise" in 1905, a "Comparative Study of the Negro Problem" in 1899, Love's "Disfranchisement of the Negro" in 1899, Grimke's Study of Denmark Vesey in 1901 and Steward's "Black St. Domingo Legion" in 1899. Since 1900 the stream of Negro writing has continued. Dunbar has found a successor in the critic and compiler of anthologies, W. S. Braithwaite; Booker T. Washington has given us his biography and Story of the Negro; Kelly Miller's trenchant essays have appeared in book form and he has issued numbers of critical monographs on the Negro problem with wide circulation. Scientific historians have appeared in Benjamin Brawley and Carter Woodson and George W. Mitchell. Sinclair's Aftermath of Slavery has attracted attention, as have the studies made by Atlanta University. The Negro in American Sculpture has been studied by H. F. M. Murray.

The development in poetry has been significant, beginning with Phyllis Wheatley.[7] Jupiter Hammon came in the 18th century, George M. Horton in the early part of the 19th century followed by Frances Harper who began publishing in 1854 and A. A. Whitman whose first attempts at epic poetry were published in the seventies. In 1890 came the first thin volume of Paul Lawrence Dunbar, the undoubted laureate of the race, who published poems and one or two novels up until the beginning of the 20th century. He was succeeded by William Stanley Braithwaite whose fame rests chiefly upon his poetic criticism and his anthologies, and finally by James Weldon Johnson,

---

7. A. A. Schomberg, *A Bibliographical Checklist of American Negro Poetry,* New York, 1916.

Claud McKay who came out of the West Indies with a new and sincere gift, Fenton Johnson, Georgia Johnson and Jessie Fauset. Joseph S. Cotter, Jr., Langston Hughes, Roscoe C. Jamison and Countée Cullen have done notable work in verse. Campbell, Davis and others have continued the poetic tradition of Negro dialect.

On the whole, the literary output of the American Negro has been both large and creditable, although, of course, comparatively little known; few great names have appeared and only here and there work that could be called first class, but this is not a peculiarity of Negro literature.

The time has not yet come for the great development of American Negro literature. The economic stress is too great and the racial persecution too bitter to allow the leisure and the poise for which literature calls. "The Negro in the United States is consuming all his intellectual energy in this gruelling race-struggle. And the same statement may be made in a general way about the white South. Why does not the white South produce literature and art? The white South, too, is consuming all of its intellectual energy in this lamentable conflict. Nearly all of the mental efforts of the white South run through one narrow channel. The life of every southern white man and all of his activities are impassably limited by the ever present Negro problem. And that is why, as Mr. H. L. Mencken puts it, in all that vast region, with its thirty or forty million people and its territory as large as half a dozen Frances or Germanys, "there is not a single poet, not a serious historian, not a creditable composer, not a critic good or bad, not a dramatist dead or alive."

On the other hand, never in the world has a richer mass of material been accumulated by a people than that which the Negroes possess today and are becoming increasingly conscious of. Slowly but surely they are developing artists of technic who will be able to use this material. The nation does not notice this for everything touching the Negro has hitherto been banned by magazines and publishers unless it took the form of caricature or bitter attack, or was so thoroughly innocuous as to have no literary flavor. This attitude shows signs of change at last.

Most of the names in this considerable list except those toward the last would be unknown to the student of American literature. Nevertheless they form a fairly continuous tradition and a most valuable group expression. From them several have arisen, as I have said, to become figures in the main stream of American literature. Phyllis Wheatley was an American writer of Negro descent just as Dumas was a French writer of Negro descent. She was the peer of her best American contemporaries but she represented no conscious Negro group. Lemuel Haynes wrote for Americans rather than for Negroes.

Dunbar occupies a unique place in American literature. He raised a dialect and a theme from the minstrel stage to literature and became and remains a national figure. Charles W. Chesnutt followed him as a novelist, and many white people read in form of fiction a subject which they did not want to read or hearken to. He gained his way unaided and by sheer merit and is a recognized American novelist. Braithwaite is a critic whose Negro descent is not generally known and has but slightly influenced his work. His place in American literature is due more to his work as a critic and anthologist than to his work as a poet. "There is still another role he has played, that of friend of poetry and poets. It is a recognized fact that in the work which preceded the present revival of poetry in the United States, no one rendered more unremitting and valuable service than Mr. Braithwaite. And it can be said that no future study of American poetry of this age can be made without reference to Braithwaite."

Of McKay's poems, Max Eastman writes that it "should be illuminating to observe that while these poems are characteristic of that race as we most admire it—they are gentle, simple, candid, brave and friendly, quick of laughter and of tears—yet they are still more characteristic of what is deep and universal in mankind. There is no special or exotic kind of merit in them, no quality that demands a transmutation of our own natures to perceive. Just as the sculptures and wood and ivory carvings of the vast forgotten African Empires of Ife and Benin, although so wistful in their tranquility, are tranquil in the possession of the qualities of all classic and great art, so these poems, the purest of them, move with a sovereignty that is never new to the lovers of the high music of human utterance."[8]

The later writers like Jean Toomer, Claud McKay, Jessie Fauset and others have come on the stage when the stream of Negro literature has grown to be of such importance and gained so much of technique and merit that it tends to merge into the broad flood of American literature and any notable Negro writer became *ipso facto* a national writer.

One must not forget the Negro orator. While in the white world the human voice as a vehicle of information and persuasion has waned in

---

8. Preface to Claud McKay's *Harlem Shadows*.

W.E.B. DU BOIS

importance until the average man is somewhat suspicious of "eloquence," in the Negro world the spoken word is still dominant and Negro orators have wielded great influence upon both white and black from the time of Frederick Douglass and Samuel Ward down to the day of J. C. Price and Booker T. Washington. There is here, undoubtedly, something of unusual gift and personal magnetism.

One must note in this connection the rise and spread of a Negro press—magazines and weeklies which are voicing to the world with increasing power the thought of American Negroes. The influence of this new force in America is being recognized and the circulation of these papers aggregate more than a million copies.

On the stage the Negro has naturally had a most difficult chance to be recognized. He has been portrayed by white dramatists and actors, and for a time it seemed but natural for a character like Othello to be drawn, or for Southerne's Oroonoko to be presented in 1696 in England with a black Angola prince as its hero. Beginning, however, with the latter part of the 18th century the stage began to make fun of the Negro and the drunken character Mungo was introduced at Drury Lane.

In the United States this tradition was continued by the "Negro Minstrels" which began with Thomas D. Rice's imitation of a Negro cripple, Jim Crow. Rice began his work in Louisville in 1828 and had great success. Minstrel companies imitating Negro songs and dances and blackening their faces gained a great vogue until long after the Civil War. Negroes themselves began to appear as principals in minstrel companies after a time and indeed as early as 1820 there was an "African company" playing in New York. No sooner had the Negro become the principal in the minstrel shows than he began to develop and uplift the art. This took a long time but eventually there appeared Cole and Johnson, Ernest Hogan and Williams and Walker. Their development of a new light comedy marked an epoch and Bert Williams was at his recent death without doubt the leading comedian on the American stage.

In the legitimate drama there was at first no chance for the Negro in the United States. Ira Aldridge, born in Maryland, had to go to Europe for opportunity. There he became associated with leading actors like Edmund Keene and was regarded in the fifties as one of the two or three greatest actors in the world. He was honored and decorated by the King of Sweden, the King of Prussia, the Emperor of Austria and the Czar of Russia. He had practically no successor until Charles Gilpin triumphed in "The Emperor Jones" in New York during the season 1920–21.

Efforts to develop a new distinctly racial drama and portray the dramatic struggle of the Negro in America and elsewhere have rapidly been made. Mrs. Emily Hapgood made determined effort to initiate a Negro theatre. She chose the plays of Ridgeley Torrence, a white playwright, who wrote for the Negro players "Granny Maumee" and "The Rider of Dreams," pieces singularly true to Negro genius. The plays were given with unusual merit and gained the highest praise.

This movement, interrupted by the war, has been started again by the Ethiopian Players of Chicago and especially by the workers at Howard University where a Negro drama with Negro instructors, Negro themes and Negro players is being developed. One of the most interesting pageants given in America was written, staged and performed by Negroes in New York, Philadelphia and Washington.

Charles Gilpin had been trained with Williams and Walker and other colored companies. He got his first chance on the legitimate stage by playing the part of Curtis in Drinkwater's "Abraham Lincoln." Then he became the principal in O'Neill's wonderful play and was nominated by the Drama League in 1921 as one of the ten persons who had contributed most to the American theatre during the year. Paul Robeson and Evelyn Preer are following Gilpin's footsteps.

There is no doubt of the Negro's dramatic genius. Stephen Graham writes:

"I visited one evening a Negro theatre where a musical comedy was going on—words and music both by Negroes. It opened with the usual singing and dancing chorus of Negro girls. They were clad in yellow and crimson and mauve combinations with white tapes on one side from the lace edge of the knicker to their dusky arms. They danced from the thigh rather than from the knee, moving waist and bosom in unrestrained undulation, girls with large, startled seeming eyes and uncontrollable masses of dark hair. A dance of physical joy and abandon, with no restraint in the toes or the knees, no veiling of the eyes, no half shutting of the lips, no holding in of the hair. Accustomed to the very aesthetic presentment of the Bacchanalia in the Russian ballet, it might be difficult to call one of those Negro dancers a Bacchante, and yet there was one whom I remarked again and again, a Queen of Sheba in her looks, a face like starry night, and she was clad slightly in mauve, and went into such ecstacies during the many encores that her hair fell down about her bare shoulders, and her cheeks and knees, glistening with perspiration, outshone her eyes. . . I had seen nothing so pretty or so amusing, so bewilderingly full of life and color, since Sanine's production of the 'Fair of Sorochinsky' in Moscow."

Turning now to painting, we note a young African painter contemporary with Phyllis Wheatley who had gained some little renown. Then a half century ago came E. M. Banister, the center of a group of artists forming the Rhode Island Art Club, and one of whose pictures took a medal at the Centennial Exposition in 1876.

William A. Harper died in 1910. His "Avenue of Poplars" took a prize of $100 at the Chicago Art Institute. William Edward Scott studied in Paris under Tanner. His picture "La Pauvre Voisine" was hung in the salon in 1910 and bought by the government of the Argentine Republic. Another picture was hung in Paris and took first prize at the Indiana State Fair, and a third picture was exhibited in the Royal Academy in London. Lately Mr. Scott has specialized in mural painting. His work is found in ten public schools in Chicago, in four in Indianapolis and in the latter city he decorated two units in the City Hospital with 300 life sized pictures. In many of these pictures he has especially emphasized the Negro type.

Richard Brown, Edwin Harleston, Albert A. Smith, Laura Wheeler and a number of rising young painters have shown the ability of the Negro in this line of art; but their dean is, of course, Henry Ossawa Tanner. Tanner is today one of the leading painters of the world and universally is so recognized. He was born an American Negro in Pittsburgh in 1859, the son of an African Methodist minister; he studied at the Academy of Fine Arts in Philadelphia and became a photographer in Atlanta. Afterward he taught at Clark University in Atlanta. In all this time he had sold less than $200 worth of pictures; but finally he got to Paris and was encouraged by Benjamin Constant. He soon turned toward his greatest forte, religious pictures. His "Daniel in the Lion's Den" was hung in the salon in 1896 and the next year the "Raising of Lazarus" was bought by the French government and hung in the Luxembourg. Since then he has won medals in all the greatest expositions, and his works are sought by connoisseurs. He has recently received knighthood in the French Legion of Honor.

In sculpture we may again think of two points of view,—first, there is the way in which the Negro type has figured in American sculpture as, for instance, the libyan Sybil of W. A. Story, Bissell's Emancipation group in Scotland, the Negro woman on the military monument in Detroit, Ball's Negro in the various emancipation groups, Ward's colored woman on the Beecher monument, the panel on the Cleveland monument of Scofield, Africa in D. C. French's group in front of the Custom's House in New York City, Calder's black boy in the Nations of the West group in the Panama-Pacific exhibition and, of course, the celebrated Shaw monument in Boston.[9] On the other hand, there have been a few Negro sculptors, three of whom merit mention: Edmonia Lewis, who worked during the Civil War, Meta Warrick Fuller, a pupil of Rodin, and May Howard Jackson, who has done some wonderful work in the portraying of the mulatto type.

To appraise rightly this body of art one must remember that it represents mainly the work of those artists whom accident set free; if the artist had a white face his Negro blood did not militate against him in the fight for recognition; if his Negro blood was visible white relatives may have helped him; in a few cases ability was united to indomitable will. But the shrinking, modest, black artist without special encouragement had little or no chance in a world determined to make him a menial. Today the situation is changing. The Negro world is demanding expression in art and beginning to pay for it. The white world is able to see dimly beyond the color line. This sum of accomplishment then is but a beginning and an imperfect indication of what the Negro race is capable of in America and in the world.

Science, worse luck, has in these drab days little commerce with art and yet for lack of better place a word may drop here of the American Negro's contribution. Science today is a matter chiefly for endowed fellowships and college chairs. Negroes have small chance here because of race exclusion and yet no scientist in the world can today write of insects and ignore the work of C. H. Turner of St. Louis; or of insanity and forget Dr. S. C. Fuller of Massachusetts. Ernest Just's investigations of the origin of life make him stand among the highest two or three modern scientists in that line and the greatest American interpreter of Wasserman reactions is a colored man; Dr. Julien H. Lewis of the University of Chicago, is building a reputation in serology. There are also a number of deft Negro surgeons including Dr. Dan Williams who first sewed up a wounded human heart. The great precursors of all these colored men of science were Thomas Derham and Benjamin Banneker.

9. Cf. Freeman H. M. Murray, *Emancipation and the Freed in American Sculpture,* Washington, D. C., 1916.

Derham was a curiosity more than a great scientist measuring by absolute standards, and yet in the 18th century and at the age of twenty-six he was regarded as one of the most eminent physicians in New Orleans. Dr. Rush of Philadelphia testified to his learning and ability.

Benjamin Banneker was a leading American scientist. He was the grandson of an English woman and her black slave. Their daughter married a Negro and Benjamin was their only son. Born in 1731 in Maryland he was educated in a private school with whites and spent his life on his father's farm. He had taste for mathematics and early constructed an ingenious clock. He became expert in the solution of difficult mathematical problems, corresponding with interested persons of leisure.

Thomas Jefferson wrote to the Marquis de Condorcet: "We now have in the United States a Negro, the son of a black man born in Africa and a black woman born in the United States, who is a very respectable mathematician. I procured him to be employed under one of our chief directors in laying out the new Federal City on the Potomac and in the intervals of his leisure, while on that work, he made an almanac for the next year, which he sent me in his own handwriting and which I enclose to you. I have seen very elegant solutions of geometrical problems by him. Add to this that he is a very worthy and respectable member of society. He is a free man. I shall be delighted to see these instances of moral eminence so multiplied as to prove that the want of talents observed in them, is merely the effect of their degraded condition, and not proceeding from any difference in the structure of the parts on which intellect depends."[10]

Banneker became greatly interested in astronomy. He made a number of calculations and finally completed an almanac covering the year 1792. A member of John Adams' cabinet had this almanac published in Baltimore. This patron, James McHenry, said that the almanac was begun and finished without outside assistance except the loan of books "so that whatever merit is attached to his present performance, is exclusively and peculiarly his own." The publishers declared that the almanac met the approbation of several of the most distinguished astronomers of America. The almanac was published yearly until 1802.

---

10. *Journal of Negro History,* Vol. 3, p. 99ff. Later, Jefferson writing to an American thought Banneker had "a mind of very common stature indeed".

When the City of Washington was laid out in 1793 under Major Pierre Charles L'Enfant, President Washington at the suggestion of Thomas Jefferson appointed Banneker as one of the six commissioners. He performed a most important part of the mathematical calculations of the survey and sat in conference with the other commissioners. Later he wrote essays on bees and studied methods to promote peace, suggesting a Secretary of Peace in the president's cabinet. He "was a brave looking pleasant man with something very noble in his appearance." His color was not jet black but decided Negroid. He died in 1806, with both an American and European reputation and was among the most learned men of his day in America.

IX

The Gift of the Spirit

How the fine sweet spirit of black folk, despite superstition and passion has breathed the soul of humility and forgiveness into the formalism and cant of American religion.

Above and beyond all that we have mentioned, perhaps least tangible but just as true, is the peculiar spiritual quality which the Negro has injected into American life and civilization. It is hard to define or characterize it—a certain spiritual joyousness; a sensuous, tropical love of life, in vivid contrast to the cool and cautious New England reason; a slow and dreamful conception of the universe, a drawling and slurring of speech, an intense sensitiveness to spiritual values—all these things and others like to them, tell of the imprint of Africa on Europe in America. There is no gainsaying or explaining away this tremendous influence of the contact of the north and south, of black and white, of Anglo Saxon and Negro.

One way this influence has been brought to bear is through the actual mingling of blood. But this is the smaller cause of Negro influence. Heredity is always stronger through the influence of acts and deeds and imitations than through actual blood descent; and the presence of the Negro in the United States quite apart from the mingling of blood has always strongly influenced the land. We have spoken of its influence in politics, literature and art, but we have yet to speak of that potent influence in another sphere of the world's spiritual activities: religion.

America early became a refuge for religion—a place of mighty spaces and glorious physical and mental freedom where silent men might sit and think quietly of God and his world. Hither out of the blood and dust of war-wrecked Europe with its jealousies, blows, persecutions and fear of words and thought, came Puritans, Anabaptists, Catholics, Quakers, Moravians, Methodists—all sorts of men and "isms" and sects searching for God and Truth in the lonely bitter wilderness.

Hither too came the Negro. From the first he was the concrete test of that search for Truth, of the strife toward a God, of that body of belief which is the essence of true religion. His presence rent and tore and tried the souls of men. "Away with the slave!" some cried—but where away and why? Was not his body there for work and his soul—what of his soul? Bring hither the slaves of all Africa and let us convert their souls, this is God's good reason for slavery. But convert them to what? to freedom? to emancipation? to being white men? Impossible. Convert them, yes. But let them still be slaves for their own good and ours. This was quibbling and good men felt it, but at least here was a practical path, follow it.

Thus arose the great mission movements to the blacks. The Catholic Church began it and not only were there Negro proselytes but black priests and an order of black monks in Spanish America early in the 16th century. In the middle of the 17th century a Negro freedman and charcoal burner lived to see his son, Francisco Xavier de Luna Victoria, raised to head the Bishopric of Panama where he reigned eight years as the first native Catholic Bishop in America.

In Spanish America and in French America the history of Negro religion is bound up with the history of the Catholic Church. On the other hand in the present territory of the United States with the exception of Maryland and Louisiana organized religion was practically and almost exclusively Protestant and Catholics indeed were often bracketed with Negroes for persecution. They could not marry Protestants at one time in colonial South Carolina; Catholics and Negroes could not appear in court as witnesses in Virginia by the law of 1705; Negroes and Catholics were held to be the cause of the "Negro plot" in New York in 1741.

The work then of the Catholic Church among Negroes began in the United States well into the 19th century and by Negroes themselves. In Baltimore, for instance, in 1829, colored refugees from the French West Indies established a sisterhood and academy and gave an initial endowment of furniture, real estate and some $50,000 in money. In 1842 in New Orleans, four free Negro women gave their wealth to form the Sisters of the Holy Family and this work expanded and grew especially after 1893 when a mulatto, Thomy Lafon, endowed the work with over three quarters of a million dollars, his life savings. Later, in 1896, a colored man, Colonel John McKee of Philadelphia, left a million dollars in real estate to the Catholic Church for colored and white orphans.

Outside of these colored sisterhoods and colored philanthropists, the church hesitated long before it began any systematic proselyting among Negroes. This was because of the comparative weakness of the church in early days and later when the Irish migration strengthened it the new Catholics were thrown into violent economic competition with slaves and free Negroes, and their fight to escape slave competition easily resolved itself into a serious anti-Negro hatred which was back of much of the rioting in Cincinnati, Philadelphia and New York. It was not then until the 20th century that the church began active work by establishing a special mission for Negroes and engaging in it nearly two hundred white priests. This new impetus was caused by the benevolence of Katherine Drexel and the Sisters of the Blessed Sacrament. Notwithstanding all this and since the beginning of the 18th century only six Negroes have been ordained to the Catholic priesthood.

The main question of the conversion of the Negro to Christianity in the United States was therefore the task of the Protestant Church and it was, if the truth must be told, a task which it did not at all relish. The whole situation was fraught with perplexing contradictions; Could Christians be slaves? Could slaves be Christians? Was the object of slavery the Christianizing of the black man, and when the black man was Christianized was the mission of slavery done and ended? Was it possible to make modern Christians of these persons whom the new slavery began to paint as brutes? The English Episcopal Church finally began the work in 1701 through the Society for the Propagation of the Gospel. It had notable officials, the Archbishop of Canterbury being its first president; it worked in America 82 years, accomplishing something but after all not very much, on account of the persistent objection of the masters. The Moravians were more eager and sent missionaries to the Negroes, converting large numbers in the West Indies and some in the United States in the 18th century. Into the new Methodist Church which came to America in 1766, large numbers of Negroes poured from the first, and finally the Baptists in the 18th century had at least one fourth of their membership composed of Negroes, so that in 1800 there were 14,000 black Methodists and some 20,000 black Baptists.[1]

It must not be assumed that this missionary work acted on raw material. Rather it reacted and was itself influenced by a very definite and important body of thought and belief on the part of the Negroes. Religion in the United States was not simply brought to the Negro by the missionaries. To treat it in that way is to miss the essence of the

---

1. Charles C. Jones, *Religious Instruction of the Negroes,* Savannah, 1842.

Negro action and reaction upon American religion. We must think of the transplanting of the Negro as transplanting to the United States a certain spiritual entity, and an unbreakable set of world-old beliefs, manners, morals, superstitions and religious observances. The religion of Africa is the universal animism or fetishism of primitive peoples, rising to polytheism and approaching monotheism chiefly, but not wholly, as a result of Christian and Islamic missions. Of fetishism there is much misapprehension. It is not mere senseless degradation. It is a philosophy of life. Among primitive Negroes there can be, as Miss Kingsley reminds us, no such divorce of religion from practical life as is common in civilized lands. Religion is life, and fetish an expression of the practical recognition of dominant forces in which the Negro lives. To him all the world is spirit. Miss Kingsley says: "It is this power of being able logically to account for everything that is, I believe, at the back of the tremendous permanency of fetish in Africa, and the cause of many of the relapses into it by Africans converted to other religions; it is also the explanation of the fact that white men who live in the districts where death and danger are everyday affairs, under a grim pall of boredom, are liable to believe in fetish, though ashamed of so doing. For the African, whose mind has been soaked in fetish during his early and most impressionable years, the voice of fetish is almost irresistible when affliction comes to him."[2]

At first sight it would seem that slavery completely destroyed every vestige of spontaneous social movement among the Negroes; the home had deteriorated; political authority and economic initiative was in the hands of the masters; property, as a social institution, did not exist on the plantation; and, indeed, it is usually assumed by historians and sociologists that every vestige of internal development disappeared, leaving the slaves no means of expression for their common life, thought, and striving. This is not strictly true; the vast power of the priest in the African state still survived; his realm alone—the province of religion and medicine—remained largely unaffected by the plantation system in many important particulars. The Negro priest, therefore, early became an important figure on the plantation and found his function as the interpreter of the supernatural, the comforter of the sorrowing, and as the one who expressed, rudely, but picturesquely, the longing and disappointment and resentment of a stolen people. From such beginnings arose and spread with marvellous rapidity the Negro church,

---

2. M. H. Kingsley, *West African Studies.*

W.E.B. DU BOIS

the first distinctively Negro American social institution. It was not at first by any means a Christian Church, but a mere adaptation of those heathen rites which we roughly designate by the term Obe Worship or "Voodooism." Association and missionary effort soon gave these rites a veneer of Christianity, and gradually, after two centuries, the Church became Christian, with a simple Calvinistic creed, but with many of the old customs still clinging to the services. It is this historic fact that the Negro Church today bases itself upon the sole surviving social institution of the African fatherland, that accounts for its extraordinary growth and vitality. We easily forget that in the United States today there is a Church organization for every sixty Negro families. This institution, therefore, naturally assumed many functions which the other harshly suppressed social organs had to surrender; the Church became the center of amusements, of what little spontaneous economic activity remained, of education, and of all social intercourse, of music and art.[3]

For these reasons the tendency of the Negro worshippers from the very first was to integrate into their own organizations. As early as 1775 distinct Negro congregations with Negro ministers began to appear here and there in the United States. They multiplied, were swept away, effort was made to absorb them in the white church, but they kept on growing until they established national bodies with Episcopal control or democratic federation and these organizations today form the strongest, most inclusive and most vital of the Negro organizations. They count in the United States four million members and their churches seat these four million and six million other guests. They are houses in 40,000 centers, worth $60,000,000 and have some 200,000 leaders.

On the part of the white church this tendency among the Negroes met with alternate encouragement and objection: encouragement because they did not want Negroes in their churches even when they occupied the back seats or in the gallery; objection when the church became, as it so often did, a center of intelligent Negro life and even of plotting against slavery. There arose out of the church the first leaders of the Negro group; and in the first rank among these stands Richard Allen.[4]

Richard Allen was born in 1760 as a slave in Philadelphia and was licensed to preach in 1782. He was ordained deacon by Bishop Asbury

---

3. Atlanta University Publications, *The Negro Church*, 1903.
4. Richard Allen, *Life, Experience and Gospel Labors*, Philadelphia, 1880.

and he led the Negroes in their secession from St. George's Church in Philadelphia when they tried to stop black folk from praying on the main floor. He formed first the Free African Society and finally established Bethel Church.

As this church grew and multiplied it became the African Methodist Episcopal Church which now boasts three quarters of a million members. Allen was its first bishop. With Allen was associated Absalom Jones, born a slave in Delaware in 1746. He became the first Negro priest in the Episcopal Church. John Gloucester became the pioneer Negro minister among colored Presbyterians and gave that church his four sons as ministers. George Leile became a missionary of the American Negroes to the Negroes of Jamaica and began missionary work on that island while Lott Carey in a similar way became a missionary to Africa. Then came Nat Turner, the preacher revolutionist. James Varick, a free negro of New York who was the first bishop of the black Zion Methodist revolt, and afterward there followed the stream of Negro leaders who have built and led the organization of colored churches. But this is only part of the story.

It will be seen that the development of the Negro church was not separate from the white. Black preachers led white congregations, white preachers addressed blacks. In many other ways Negroes influenced white religion continuously and tremendously. There was the "Shout," combining the trance and demoniac possession as old as the world, and revivified and made wide-spread by the Negro religious devotees in America. Methodist and Baptist ways of worship, songs and religious dances absorbed much from the Negroes and whatever there is in American religion today of stirring and wild enthusiasm, of loud conversions and every day belief in an anthropomorphic God owes its origin in a no small measure to the black man.

Of course most of the influence of the Negro preachers was thrown into their own churches and to their own people and it was from the Negro church as an organization that Negro religious influence spread most widely to white people. Many would say that this influence had little that was uplifting and was a detriment rather than an advantage in that it held back and holds back the South particularly in its religious development. There is no doubt that influences of a primitive sort and customs that belong to the unlettered childhood of the race rather than to the thinking adult life of civilization crept in with the religious influence of the slave. Much of superstition, even going so far as witchcraft, conjury and blood sacrifice for a long time marked Negro religion here and there in the swamps and islands. But on the other hand it is just as true that the cold formalism of upper class England and New England needed the wilder spiritual emotionalism of the black man to weld out of both a rational human religion based on kindliness and social uplift; and whether the influence of Negro religion was on the whole good or bad, the fact remains that it was potent in the white South and still is.

Several black leaders of white churches are worth remembering.[5] Lemuel Hayes was born in Connecticut in 1753 of a black father and white mother. He received his Master of Arts from Middlebury College in 1804, was a soldier in the Revolution and pastored various churches in New England. "He was the embodiment of piety and honesty." Harry Hosier, the black servant and companion of Bishop Asbury, was called by Dr. Benjamin Rush, the greatest orator in America. He travelled north and south and preached to white and black between 1784 and his death in 1810.

John Chavis was a full-blooded Negro, born in Granville county, N. C., near Oxford, in 1753. He was born free and was sent to Princeton, and studied privately under Dr. Witherspoon, where he did well. He went to Virginia to preach to Negroes. In 1802, in the county court, his freedom and character were certified to and it was declared that he had passed "through a regular course of academic studies" at what is now Washington and Lee University. In 1805 he returned to North Carolina, where he, in 1809 was made a licentiate in the Presbyterian Church and preached. His English was remarkably pure, his manner impressive, his explanations clear and concise. For a long time he taught school and had the best whites as pupils—a United States senator, the sons of a chief justice of North Carolina, a governor of the state and many others. Some of his pupils boarded in his family, and his school was regarded as the best in the State. "All accounts agree that John Chavis was a gentleman" and he was received socially among the best whites and asked to table. In 1830 he was stopped from preaching by the law. Afterward he taught school for free Negroes in Raleigh.

Henry Evans was a full-blooded Virgina free Negro, and was the pioneer of Methodism in Fayetteville, N. C. He found the Negroes there,

---

5. Cf. Carter G. Woodson, *The History of the Negro Church*, Washington, D. C., 1921; Atlanta University Publications, *The Negro Church*; and J. E. Bassett, *Slavery in North Carolina*.

about 1800, without religious instruction. He began preaching and the town council ordered him away; he continued and whites came to hear him. Finally the white auditors outnumbered the black, and sheds were erected for Negroes at the side of the church. The gathering became a regular Methodist Church, with a white and Negro membership, but Evans continued to preach. He exhibited "rare self-control before the most wretched of castes! Henry Evans did much good, but he would have done more good had his spirit been untrammelled by this sense of inferiority."[6]

His dying words uttered as he stood, aged and bent beside his pulpit, are of singular pathos:

"I have come to say my last word to you. It is this: None but Christ. Three times I have had my life in jeopardy for preaching the gospel to you. Three times I have broken ice on the edge of the water and swam across the Cape Fear to preach the gospel to you; and, if in my last hour I could trust to that, or anything but Christ crucified, for my salvation, all should be lost and my soul perish forever."

Early in the nineteenth century, Ralph Freeman was a slave in Anson county, N. C. He was a full-blooded Negro, and was ordained and became an able Baptist preacher. He baptised and administered communion, and was greatly respected. When the Baptists split on the question of missions he sided with the anti-mission side. Finally the law forbade him to preach.

The story of Jack of Virginia is best told in the words of a Southern writer:

"Probably the most interesting case in the whole South is that of an African preacher of Nottoway county, popularly known as 'Uncle Jack,' whose services to white and black were so valuable that a distinguished minister of the Southern Presbyterian Church felt called upon to memorize his work in a biography.

"Kidnapped from his idolatrous parents in Africa, he was brought over in one of the last cargoes of slaves admitted to Virginia and sold to a remote and obscure planter in Nottoway county, a region at that time in the backwoods and destitute particularly as to religious life and instruction. He was converted under the occasional preaching of Rev. Dr. John Blair Smith, President of Hampden-Sidney College, and of Dr. William Hill and Dr. Archibald Alexander of Princeton, then

---

6. Bassett, pp. 58–9.

young theologues, and by hearing the scriptures read. Taught by his master's children to read, he became so full of the spirit and knowledge of the Bible that he was recognized among the whites as a powerful expounder of Christian doctrine, was licensed to preach by the Baptist Church, and preached from plantation to plantation within a radius of thirty miles, as he was invited by overseers or masters. His freedom was purchased by a subscription of whites, and he was given a home and a tract of land for his support. He organized a large and orderly Negro church, and exercised such a wonderful controlling influence over the private morals of his flock that masters, instead of punishing their slaves, often referred them to the discipline of their pastor, which they dreaded far more.

"He stopped a heresy among the Negro Christians of Southern Virginia, defeating in open argument a famous fanatical Negro preacher named Campbell, who advocated noise and 'the spirit' against the Bible, winning over Campbell's adherents in a body. For over forty years and until he was nearly a hundred years of age, he labored successfully in public and private among black and whites, voluntarily giving up his preaching in obedience to the law of 1832, the result of 'Old Nat's war.' . . .

"The most refined and aristocratic people paid tribute to him, and he was instrumental in the conversion of many whites. Says his biographer, Rev. Dr. William S. White: 'He was invited into their houses, sat with their families, took part in their social worship, sometimes leading the prayer at the family altar. Many of the most intelligent people attended upon his ministry and listened to his sermons with great delight. Indeed, previous to the year 1825, he was considered by the best judges to be the best preacher in that county. His opinions were respected, his advice followed, and yet he never betrayed the least symptoms of arrogance or self-conceit. His dwelling was a rude log cabin, his apparel of the plainest and coarsest materials.' This was because he wished to be fully identified with his class. He refused gifts of better clothing saying 'These clothes are a great deal better than are generally worn by people of my color, and besides if I wear them I find shall be obliged to think about them even at meeting'."

All this has to do with organized religion.

But back of all this and behind the half childish theology of formal religion there has run in the heart of black folk the greatest of human achievements, love and sympathy, even for their enemies, for those who despised them and hurt them and did them nameless ill. They have nursed the sick and closed the staring eyes of the dead. They have given friendship to the friendless, they have shared the pittance of their poverty with the outcast and nameless; they have been good and true and pitiful to the bad and false and pitiless and in this lies the real grandeur of their simple religion, the mightiest gift of black to white America.

Above all looms the figure of the Black Mammy, one of the most pitiful of the world's Christs. Whether drab and dirty drudge or dark and gentle lady she played her part in the uplift of the South. She was an embodied Sorrow, an anomaly crucified on the cross of her own neglected children for the sake of the children of masters who bought and sold her as they bought and sold cattle. Whatever she had of slovenliness or neatness, of degradation or of education she surrendered it to those who lived to lynch her sons and ravish her daughters. From her great full breast walked forth governors and judges, ladies of wealth and fashions, merchants and scoundrels who lead the South. And the rest gave her memory the reverence of silence. But a few snobs have lately sought to advertise her sacrifice and degradation and enhance their own cheap success by building on the blood of her riven heart a load of stone miscalled a monument.

In religion as in democracy, the Negro has been a peculiar test of white profession. The American church, both Catholic and Protestant, has been kept from any temptation to over-righteousness and empty formalism by the fact that just as Democracy in America was tested by the Negro, so American religion has always been tested by slavery and color prejudice. It has kept before America's truer souls the spirit of meekness and self abasement, it has compelled American religion again and again to search its heart and cry "I have sinned;" and until the day comes when color caste falls before reason and economic opportunity the black American will stand as the last and terrible test of the ethics of Jesus Christ.

Beyond this the black man has brought to America a sense of meekness and humility which America never has recognized and perhaps never will. If there is anybody in this land who thoroughly believes that the meek shall inherit the earth they have not often let their presence be known. On the other hand it has become almost characteristic of America to look upon position, self assertion, determination to go forward at all odds, as typifying the American spirit. This is natural. It is at once the rebound from European oppression and the encouragement which America offers physically, economically and socially to the human spirit. But on the other hand, it is in many of its aspects a dangerous and awful thing. It hardens and hurts our souls, it contradicts our philanthropy and religion; and here it is that the honesty of the black race, its hesitancy and heart searching, its submission to authority and its deep sympathy with the wishes of the other man comes forward as a tremendous, even though despised corrective. It is not always going to remain; even now we see signs of its disappearance before contempt, lawlessness and lynching. But it is still here, it still works and one of the most magnificent anomalies in modern human history is the labor and fighting of a half-million black men and two million whites for the freedom of four million slaves and these same slaves, dumbly but faithfully and not wholly unconsciously, protecting the mothers, wives and children of the very white men who fought to make their slavery perpetual.

This then is the Gift of Black Folk to the new world. Thus in singular and fine sense the slave became master, the bond servant became free and the meek not only inherited the earth but made that heritage a thing of questing for eternal youth, of fruitful labor, of joy and music, of the free spirit and of the ministering hand, of wide and poignant sympathy with men in their struggle to live and love which is, after all, the end of being.

Postscript

Listen to the Winds, O God the Reader, that wail across the whip-cords stretched taut on broken human hearts; listen to the Bones, the bare bleached bones of slaves, that line the lanes of Seven Seas and beat eternal tom-toms in the forests of the laboring deep; listen to the Blood, the cold thick blood that spills its filth across the fields and flowers of the Free; listen to the Souls that wing and thrill and weep and scream and sob and sing above it all. What shall these things mean, O God the Reader? You know. You know.

A Note About the Author

W.E.B. Du Bois (1868–1963) was an African American sociologist, historian, civil rights activist, and socialist. Born in Massachusetts, he was raised in Great Barrington, an integrated community. He studied at the University of Berlin and at Harvard, where he became the first African American scholar to earn a doctorate. He worked as a professor at Atlanta University, a historically black institution, and was one of the leaders of the Niagara Movement, which advocated for equal rights and opposed Booker T. Washington's Atlanta compromise. In 1909, he cofounded the NAACP and served for years as the editor of its official magazine *The Crisis*. In addition to his activism against lynching, Jim Crow laws, and other forms of discrimination and segregation, Du Bois authored such influential works as *The Souls of Black Folk* (1903) and *Black Reconstruction in America* (1935). A lifelong opponent of racism and a committed pacifist, Du Bois advocated for socialism as a means of replacing racial capitalism in America and around the world. In the 1920s, he used his role at *The Crisis* to support the artists of the Harlem Renaissance and sought to emphasize the role of African Americans in shaping American society in his book *The Gift of Black Folk* (1924).

A Note from the Publisher

Spanning many genres, from non-fiction essays to literature classics to children's books and lyric poetry, Mint Edition books showcase the master works of our time in a modern new package. The text is freshly typeset, is clean and easy to read, and features a new note about the author in each volume. Many books also include exclusive new introductory material. Every book boasts a striking new cover, which makes it as appropriate for collecting as it is for gift giving. Mint Edition books are only printed when a reader orders them, so natural resources are not wasted. We're proud that our books are never manufactured in excess and exist only in the exact quantity they need to be read and enjoyed.

Discover more of your favorite classics with Bookfinity™.

- Track your reading with custom book lists.
- Get great book recommendations for your personalized Reader Type.
- Add reviews for your favorite books.
- AND MUCH MORE!

Visit **bookfinity.com** and take the fun Reader Type quiz to get started.

Enjoy our classic and modern companion pairings!